Monkey

Animal
Series editor: Jonathan Burt

Already published

Monkey

Desmond Morris

REAKTION BOOKS

Published by
REAKTION BOOKS LTD
33 Great Sutton Street
London EC1V 0DX, UK
www.reaktionbooks.co.uk

First published 2013

Printed and bound in China by C&C Offset Printing Co., Ltd

British Library Cataloguing in Publication Data
Morris, Desmond.
    Monkey. – (Animal)
    1. Monkeys.
    I. Title II. Series
    599.8-DC23

    ISBN 978 1 78023 096 2

Contents

Introduction

I recall with some embarrassment the day I walked into a shop and informed the startled young woman behind the counter that a monkey had bitten off my nipples. I asked her if she could supply me with replacements. Happily, she could and I was able to fit them back in place so that the jets from my car's windscreen washers would once again be aimed in the right direction.

For some reason, monkeys in drive-through wildlife parks love leaping on visitors' cars and causing havoc. They pull and tug and bite at anything they can get their hands around or their teeth into. In my case, it was the rubber nipples that direct the jets of water at the glass when one presses the appropriate button inside the car. Being soft and removable, they are favourite targets for the packs of captive monkeys that are so popular today in modern safari parks. Baboons in particular are adept at leaning down, clamping their large teeth on the rubber and levering the nipple loose. They chew it and spit it out before moving on to some other form of vandalism. They have done it before, of course, and they know perfectly well that the object is inedible, but they still can't resist meddling with it.

This trivial activity somehow sums up the way most people see monkeys. They are essentially mischievous beings. Indeed, the dictionary defines 'monkeying' with something as tampering with it, or playing mischievous or foolish tricks.

The face of the mandrill, with its blue cheeks, red nose and orange beard.

Monkeys in a drive-through wildlife park.

Viewed negatively, this quality of monkeys sees them as a destructive nuisance. Viewed more positively, however, it reveals them as playfully inquisitive. Herein lies their importance. For it is an undeniable fact that the most playful and inquisitive primate on the planet is the human animal. It is our playfulness, lasting well into adulthood, that has been the underlying feature of the human success story, rendering us the most powerful species on the planet. Without our playful curiosity and our endless inquisitiveness, we would never have become inventors, never have developed our amazing skills and our advanced technologies.

We are lucky that monkeys, rather than some other kind of mammals, are our remote ancestors. Because, over millions of years, we evolved from those scampering, chattering, intelligent, treetop-living creatures, we had a good starting point. Their inborn urge to explore things became the bedrock of our sophisticated innovations. Their love of activity became our industrious pursuit of knowledge.

We owe a great debt to our monkey ancestors. They set us on the right path, the path that would take us from the treetops to the moon and, one day, beyond. So they deserve a closer look.

1 Sacred Monkeys

In the West today it cannot be said that monkeys inspire reverence. We may marvel at their acrobatics in the treetops, we may admire their often striking markings and coat patterns, and we may laugh with them when they are at play, but worship them we do not. In fact, we never have. The Western world has either found them too amusing to be taken seriously, or too close to humans for comfort. In earlier centuries we have been entertained by the monkeys of street organ-grinders or we have seen them as some sort of horrid caricature of the human condition. And, of course, Darwin's earth-shattering idea that we might actually be related to them made us even more ill at ease in their presence. In other cultures, however, human attitudes towards monkeys have been entirely different.[1]

In ancient Egypt the baboon was considered a sacred being and was treated with great respect. In early India the langur monkey acquired an almost godlike status and is still worshipped to this day, despite increasing complaints from many members of modern Indian society. On the island of Bali today there is a Sacred Monkey Forest where long-tailed macaques are treated as sacred animals and allowed to roam around the temples there. In China and Japan there have been a number of monkey deities in the past and, although in modern times they have largely lost their power to inspire worship, they still play an important role in oriental folklore.

The talismanic Barbary macaques on the Rock of Gibraltar.

The only monkeys in the West that can boast any sort of mythological role are the rather sad little colonies of Barbary macaques that eke out a living on the Rock of Gibraltar. Among the human inhabitants of Gibraltar there is a firmly held belief that if the Rock Apes, as they are known, ever leave, British control of Gibraltar will end and the much disputed territory will revert to Spain. But these cannot be thought of as sacred monkeys. They are little more than lucky mascots, talismanic monkeys connected to a simple superstition. To find the true simian deities one must travel to the other end of the Mediterranean, starting in the Middle East and then moving on through Asia to the Far East.

EGYPT: THOTH, THE SACRED BABOON

The impressive figure of the male hamadryas baboon appears in many forms in the arts of ancient Egypt, from tiny figurines to huge statues and from colourful wall paintings to exquisitely

Wall painting of
sacred baboons
from the tomb
of Tutankhamun.

carved reliefs. It is usually portrayed in a squatting posture with
its heavy mane of hair enveloping its muscular body like a regal
cloak. Between its legs its long penis is usually shown in a state of
arousal, pointing straight at the onlooker, presenting a sexual
threat. Its strong jaws and solemn expression add to the intensity
of its image, making it a symbol of unchallenged power and viril-
ity. It is little wonder that the early Egyptians held it in such awe.[2]

In many cases, surviving statues have been mutilated in modern times, with the removal of the all too conspicuous penis. This is based on a misunderstanding of its significance to the sculptors who fashioned it. To them, the addition of a conspicuous phallus was an important way of displaying the baboon as the embodiment of masculine sexuality, seen as an exalted virtue in those ancient days, because the propagation of the species was viewed as man's highest duty to God.

These statues involve relatively little artistic licence. Indeed, they are remarkably true to life, for in nature the male hamadryas baboon is a startlingly impressive figure, a harem-master whose great cape of hair displays to his rivals his dominant status. He also possesses an unusually lengthy penis and spends a great deal of time sitting proudly in the squatting posture seen in so many of the Egyptian artefacts. Compared with the human penis, that of the hamadryas appears to lack a foreskin and the animal was therefore thought to be born circumcised. It has been suggested that the Egyptian priests who attended the sacred baboons honoured them by imitating this condition. In this way the ritual of human circumcision is thought to have arisen, spreading later to nearby tribes who wished to emulate the advanced Egyptians.

So strong was the Egyptian interest in the baboon penis that it was employed as the central feature of their water-clocks. Carvings of seated male baboons were created in which water flowed through a hole in the phallus, marking the hours. Bizarrely, this is because it was believed that baboons urinated regularly once every hour.

Surprisingly, although the ancient Egyptians obviously knew this large species of monkey extremely well, no baboons have ever been found living in the wild in the Egyptian countryside. Their natural habitat lies further to the south. Every baboon that existed in ancient Egypt must have been laboriously transported there as an exotic import.

Once there, it would have been taken to a temple to see if it was a suitable specimen for religious duty. According to a fifth-century BC account, a newly arrived baboon was set a curious test. It was presented with a writing tablet, a reed pen and some ink. The priests then waited to see if it showed any interest in this equipment. If it did, it was considered to be literate and was enrolled as a symbol of Thoth, the deity of scribes, of education and of the moon. In this capacity it was installed in one of the temples and was provided with fine roasted meats and wine, obtained through gifts from the worshippers.

Sadly, this lavish but highly unsuitable diet and a lack of proper exercise led to early deaths in most of these sacred animals, as has been discovered from an examination of their mummies. They lived protected, pampered lives, but died young.

In their sacred role, they developed into key figures in religious cults. At Ashmunein in Middle Egypt, one can still see dramatic evidence of the extent to which they were revered. Here, at the main centre of the cult of Thoth, sculptors were given the task of fashioning four gigantic baboon statues out of quartzite rock. Two of these figures survive. They are about 6 m (20 ft) high and weigh around 35 tons each. With the exception of the Sphinx, they are perhaps the largest animal carvings in the world, vividly underlining the importance of the baboon in the religious concepts of the ancient Egyptians.

In some wall paintings and carvings, male baboons are depicted with their arms held out, palms up, in the typical posture of ancient prayer. It was thought that in this position they would greet the moon and pray to her to ensure her presence in the heavens.

At dawn, as the moon-god Thoth gave way to the sun-god Re, baboons were believed to perform a special greeting ritual that

One of the gigantic baboon statues at Ashmunein.

involved dancing and singing. This fanciful concept has a factual basis because, in the wild, waking baboons were often seen to react to each new dawn by calling, screeching and leaping about.

Baboons that were rejected by the temple priests as unsuitable for a sacred life often ended up as high-status pets in rich Egyptian households. The idea of keeping such a dangerous animal as a household companion seems strange to us today, but the early Egyptians appear to have been masters of taming and controlling a whole range of difficult wild species. They even made misguided attempts to domesticate hyenas.

There is a carved relief from the Fifth Dynasty that shows a young man walking in the marketplace with two tame female baboons on collars and leads. One is walking behind him, with a baby clinging to her underside, while the other is in front of him, grabbing at the leg of a thief who is about to steal some food from a large basket.

Female baboons were obviously more suitable as pets than the powerful males, but they too could be given a sacred significance. There was a special reason for this. They may have lacked the impressively regal mane of the males but they demonstrated a special quality of their own that caught the attention of the Egyptians: female baboons had a menstrual cycle that lasted a month, and was therefore thought to be controlled by the moon.

An Egyptian Fifth Dynasty carved relief of a young man with two tame female baboons.

This gave them an astronomical significance and they too became associated with Thoth in his capacity as a lunar divinity.

So important were baboons in Egyptian society that when they died, they were often carefully mummified. At first they were only given wooden coffins but later they were sometimes placed in limestone sarcophagi. At Saqqara an extraordinary catacomb was found in which no fewer than 400 baboons had been buried in the Ptolemaic period.

When the bodies of these mummified monkeys were carefully studied by archaeologists a surprising discovery was made. No fewer than five species were involved. In addition to the favoured hamadryas baboons, there were also olive baboons, Barbary macaques, green monkeys and red patas monkeys. These other species were probably kept only as domestic pets and it is doubtful if they played any sacred role. Their identification from the mummified remains found in tombs is important, however, as it underlines the fact that vast areas were involved in supplying primates to the ancient Egyptian civilization. Word must have gone out far and wide in Africa that good money was to be made from supplying these exotic pets to wealthy homes along the Nile.

It is clear that, as pets, they were often greatly loved by their owners and were sometimes even buried with them. The pharaoh Tuthmosis III had his favourite baboon interred with him in his royal tomb in the Valley of the Kings. Some of these pets were given personal names that are inscribed in their tombs, but they are not the kind of names, like Jacko or Bobo, that we would use for monkeys today. To our ears they sound decidedly odd. One, for example, was given the title of 'His father awaits him' and another was called 'Thoth has come'.

Medically, the monkey mummies had some sad tales to tell. Many of these much-loved animals had rickets, revealing that the Egyptians failed to understand primate dietary needs. Others had decaying teeth, or arthritis. After suffering lengthy and no doubt painful journeys from their distant homelands, the survivors would soon find themselves killed by kindness of a mistaken kind.

In India, Hanuman represents the peak of monkey prestige. No legendary monkey has ever played such a distinguished role in mythology. In the Hindu religion he is a monkey god who is seen as a noble hero, a provider of courage, hope, knowledge, intellect and devotion, and a symbol of physical strength and perseverance. In character, he is as far as it is possible to get from the sad little organ-grinder's monkey, or the wretched laboratory experiment monkey. He is an inspiration to devout Hindus, who still worship at his shrine, bring special offerings for him, chant his name and sing his hymn. But who exactly is Hanuman?

When he is portrayed he is usually shown as an adult male with a human body, but with the head and tail of a langur monkey. He is sometimes depicted holding a large mace to symbolize his bravery and he may have a picture of the great Lord Rama tattooed on his chest. In his deeds he is like a monkey-faced superman, soaring through the skies on his heroic missions. He is immensely powerful, fearless and athletic, capable of changing his size if necessary from very small to vast.

Hanuman's main role was to aid Lord Rama in his fight against evil forces, and he was assigned the task of finding Rama's abducted wife Sita. She had been kidnapped by Ravana, the wicked and lustful king of Lanka, and it was Hanuman's duty to track her down, facing enormous obstacles and obstructions along the way. His amazing feats are described in the Hindu epic called the *Ramayana*.

Hanuman the monkey god.

His first great task was to find a way to cross the sea from India to Ceylon (now renamed Sri Lanka). He and his monkey followers solved the problem by carrying huge boulders from the Himalayas down to the coast and there bridging the straits with a causeway. Great sea monsters tried to stop them, but they defeated them by changing their size. The monsters demanded that, in order to proceed, the monkeys enter their great mouths and pass right through their bodies. According to one version of the story, they did enter the mouths of the monsters but then,

Hanuman holding
a large mace.

without warning, dramatically increased their size and burst out
of the monsters' skins. In another version they became very small
and entered through the monsters' ears, afterwards escaping
through their open mouths.

The Hanuman monkeys seemed invincible. If they were killed
in battle, they were resuscitated when raindrops fell on them.
When Hanuman was eventually captured, the evil king decreed
that his tail be set on fire. When this was done, he managed to
flee by changing his size and then, trailing his burning tail behind
him, he set alight the whole of the island of Lanka, and left it in
flames, flying swiftly back to the mainland.

After further battles, Rama was finally successful and married Sita. Hanuman was offered any reward he cared to name and he chose to be able to live for as long as people spoke of the deeds of Rama. This is presumably why, to this day, the langurs of India are considered sacred and are so revered. They are grey monkeys with black faces and extremities and this colouration is said to be the result of the punishment Hanuman received when his body was set on fire.

These grey langur monkeys often become a serious pest, stealing food from gardens and raiding orchards, but no one

The langurs of India are considered sacred and are allowed to roam where they please.

dares to raise a finger against them. Anyone hurting or killing one would be liable to find themselves set upon by an angry Hindu mob. Even the cheeky rhesus monkeys that also inhabit India in large numbers are protected because, although they are not themselves considered to be sacred like the langurs, they are clearly closely related to them and therefore gain some of their mystique.

In modern times, the immunity of the langurs has led to some strange practices. In one part of India it is possible to hire men with tame monkeys to drive out the wild monkeys that are causing you trouble. No human may drive away the intruding monkeys, because that would be an attack on sacred beings, but if your trained monkey attacks them, that is between monkey and monkey and, with a little lateral thinking, it can be claimed that no human beings are involved.

If, on the other hand, you want to get even with an unpleasant human neighbour, you can enlist the help of the sacred monkeys. All you have to do is to scatter some rice on the roof of your victim's house and then sit back and wait for the monkeys to tear it apart in their attempts to find the grains lodged between the cracks.

Perhaps the most bizarre attempt at controlling the sacred monkeys involved shaving the leading male's body. The dominant male was caught with a baited trap, carefully shaved naked and then released. His shorn appearance undermined his leadership status and the troop that he had ruled soon disbanded and scattered. To the outsider this strategy might appear to be too humiliating for a sacred animal, but as no monkey was physically injured it seems to have been acceptable even to devout Hindus.

By the middle of the twentieth century, the monkey problem in India had reached epidemic proportions. It was estimated that there were no fewer than 150 million of them living in the forests

A 16th-century Indian depiction of monkeys playing.

around towns and cities. The damage they were causing was escalating annually and official demands for their control were made. The result was a cultural clash between Indians devoted to modernizing their country and those who were doggedly determined to defend ancient religious practices.

The modernists listed the outrages perpetrated by the monkeys. These included raiding shops and kitchens, stealing from street vendors, snatching personal belongings, attacking women and children, and even having the temerity to enter the offices of the Ministry of Defence, tearing up papers and holding files to ransom in exchange for sweets or pieces of fruit. Some of them fled with confidential documents and scattered them over the streets. They are so bold that they enter houses, open refrigerators and steal the contents. When angry women have chased them they are reported to have turned on their pursuers and slapped them or torn at their clothes.

In Darjeeling, a huge colony of sacred monkeys invaded a girls' college, clawed the students, broke the furniture, grabbed food from the canteen, destroyed the college library, and disrupted lessons by breaking into classrooms. In the Shastri Park area of east New Delhi, a group of monkeys went on a rampage trying to snatch infants before adults beat them back with sticks. A total of 25 people were injured. Some children were so badly bitten on the legs that they had to be taken to hospital.

On occasion, the presence of the sacred pests has led to death. In one case, they dropped a flowerpot on the head of a New Delhi resident, who died as a result. They even managed to kill the deputy mayor of Delhi. He was trying to fend off a group of monkeys that had invaded his balcony when he accidentally plunged to his death.

Despite this growing catalogue of simian outrages, religious traditionalists continue to resist any attempt to destroy the monkeys

A statue of
Hanuman over
30 metres tall
at Nandura,
Maharashtra, India.

or reduce their numbers. The problem is that the forest homes of
the animals are shrinking rapidly as the human population in India
expands and they are inevitably being driven more and more into
urban areas. In some places there is even illegal trapping of wild
forest monkeys for sale to medical research laboratories. The survivors of this onslaught flee to the cities where they are safe from
these criminal activities, if only because of the presence of devout
Hindus who will protect them. It has been estimated that 60 per
cent of the entire monkey population of India now inhabits urban
districts or the surrounding suburbs.

Clearly, in the future we will see the monkey pest problem intensifying throughout the sub-continent and sooner or later, even the most devout Hindus will eventually have to accept some sort of control of monkey numbers, or city life will become intolerable. The fact that at present the monkeys are still being allowed to cause havoc on a grand scale is a measure of the power and persistence of the Hanuman legend.

BALI: THE SACRED MONKEY FOREST

About 1,500 years ago, Hindus from India started to arrive on the small island of Bali in the centre of what is now Indonesia. Today this remains a Hindu stronghold, situated in the middle of an Indonesian population that is nearly 90 per cent Muslim. Its isolated position has, however, made its form of Hinduism rather different from that practised in India.

One feature that it does share is the acceptance of the local monkeys as venerated animals. In the Monkey Forest of Padang-tegal, a sacred Balinese Hindu site, there exist today 340 macaques,

A macaque on a statue in a sacred temple, Bali.

A macaque in the Monkey Forest of Padangtegal, Bali.

living in four warring troops, revered and protected by the local people. They are given free reign to wander over the ancient temples and when Western visitors approach the entrance to this sacred site they are bemused to find a large sign, in English, stating that menstruating women are not permitted to enter the temple area. With the monkeys urinating and defecating all over the temple buildings, it seems perverse that women should be excluded in this way, but this is simply a measure of the reverence in which these animals are held.

Traditionally, it is believed that the sacred monkeys will guard the temples against evil spirits and this is why they have to be

ATTENTION

To maintain the religious purity and cleanliness of this temple : Women during menstruation should not enter the temple. Do not climb on or deface temple structures . Wear suitable clothes and observe polite manners .

well treated even when they regularly bite visiting tourists and steal their food. It is a different matter, however, if they stray outside their sacred forest and start invading the nearby villages and rice fields. Then their status changes dramatically and they are treated by the local people as pests and dealt with accordingly. To provide an explanation as to how sacred animals can be treated in this way, it is said that they 'embody both positive and negative forces', allowing them to be revered or loathed, depending on their location.

CHINA: SUN WUKONG, THE MONKEY KING

The legendary Monkey King of China, Sun Wukong, has a magical birth in which he is hatched from an egg to become an indestructible stone monkey. On seeing him, the Pearly Emperor declares that he is destined to skip and gambol on the highest peaks of mountains, jump about in the waters and eat the fruit of the trees,

The Monkey King of China, Sun Wukong.

28

The characteristic mask of the Monkey King of China, worn by stage performers.

The operatic costume worn by the performer playing the role of the Monkey King.

and to be the finest ornament of the mountains. The other monkeys dare him to enter a cave that leads to the heavens. He is the only one who does this and is then proclaimed king by the other monkeys. He then starts to worry that one day he might die and he begins a quest for immortality. Once he has found it, the gods are too weak to control him and his exploits cause chaos and confusion. He is fearless, mischievous and irrepressible.

During his travels he learns all kinds of magic tricks. He becomes a shapeshifter, able to transform himself into 72 different kinds of beings, from trees to birds, and even to small bugs. He can fly on clouds and can travel thousands of miles in a single somersault. His favourite weapon is a magical wishing staff, acquired from the Dragon Kings, that he can expand or shrink to order.

Tripitaka and the Monkey King in a popular 1970s TV series.

Eventually the gods ask Buddha to help them and, since the Monkey King cannot be killed, Buddha encases him, trapping him under a mountain for 500 years. After this he is summoned by Buddha to act as a bodyguard and guide for a monk who must set off on a long pilgrimage. During the journey we see that the Monkey King has two special qualities – he is a playful, disobedient trickster, but he also has a good heart and always helps the monk.

This legend has been popular in China for centuries and has been made into books, operas, comic strips, cartoons, television series and films. The Sun Wukong festival is celebrated on the sixteenth day of the eighth lunar month of the Chinese calender. Some scholars see a link between China's Monkey King and India's Hanuman. In Cambodia he is, in fact, known as Hanuman Sun Wukong.

In the past the Monkey King became such an important legendary figure that some Chinese worshipped him as a god, and remnants of this reverence still cling on in some places today. In Hong Kong, for example, there is a Buddhist temple that contains a shrine to Sun Wukong.

TIBET: THE OGRESS AND THE MONKEY

In Tibet, there is a curious belief that all Tibetan people are the descendants of a mating between a female demon or ogre and a monkey. The story appears to have some echoes of the Chinese legend of the Monkey King.

The Tibetan monkey, called Pha Trelgen Changchup Sempa, has wandered into a cave in search of immortality. There, he devotes himself to a life of chaste meditation, until he is approached by Ma Drag Sinmo, a mountain ogress, who asks him to marry her. He refuses because he is a disciple of Mother Buddha and has been told to remain in the cave until he has learned and understood the Great Truths. The ogress implores him to change his mind, saying that if he does not marry her it will result in a terrible disaster for the sacred Tibetan plateau.

The monkey seeks guidance from the Mother Buddha, who tells him that it would be a kindness to marry the ogress and that

A decorated monkey skullcup from Tibet, used in Tantric rituals. Offerings to the gods are placed inside the skull.

kindness is a great virtue. So he hurries back, marries the ogress and together they produce six monkey babies. These offspring later go off into the forest looking for food. After three years have passed, their father goes in search of them, only to find that the six have now become 500. There is not enough to eat for all these monkeys, but the Mother Buddha comes to the rescue with five cereals. Using these, the father monkey creates crops that provide sufficient food for them. As time passes, they lose their tails, learn to use implements, build houses, make clothes and develop the power of speech, becoming the first Tibetans.

JAPAN: THE THREE WISE MONKEYS

The famous trio of the Three Wise Monkeys – Mizaru, covering his eyes, who sees no evil; Kikazaru, covering his ears, who hears no evil; and Iwazaru, covering his mouth, who speaks no evil – is thought to have originated in Japan. When Buddhism first reached Japan in the sixth century AD, monkey lore was already

The famous trio of the Three Wise Monkeys, a 17th-century carving above a door at the Tōshō-gū shrine in Nikkō, Japan.

The modern four Wise Monkeys.

The legacy of sacred monkeys can still be seen in modern Japan in the form of red lucky charms called *migawari-zaru*.

a common element in Buddhist legends. After this, monkey worship in Japan became increasingly popular, especially among those who performed the Taoist Kōshin rites introduced from China, and among the followers of Shintō Buddhism in the temple at Mount Hiei near Kyoto. The central deity at Mount Hiei is Sannō, representing three important Buddhas – Shaka, Yakushi and Amida – and the existence of this trio supports the idea that the three-monkeys motif may have originated there.

It is believed that the Three Wise Monkeys images were origi-nally carved on stone pillars, but one of the best of the early images that survive today is a seventeenth-century carving above a door at the Tōshō-gū shrine in Nikkō, also known as the Sacred Stable, showing red and white monkeys surrounded by brightly coloured foliage.

Recently, on curio stalls in the Far East selling small figurines of the wise monkeys, a fourth one has sometimes been added as

a joke. This one – called Shizaru, do no evil – is shown with his hands covering his genitals.

Monkey worship in Japan peaked in the Edo period, but has declined sharply since then. Even so, the legacy of sacred monkeys can still be seen in the form of red lucky charms at temples, shrines and curio shops. The colour red is said to relate to the dual role of the monkey as a protector against disease as well as a patron of fertility.

Modern monkey charms are red-and-white stuffed figures of a rather abstract form, and it is not immediately obvious that they represent monkeys. Called *migawari-zaru*, they are hung on strings near front doors, or on the eaves of a house. Each one is designated for a particular family member and is intended to absorb their misfortune. Some people make sure that their wishes are understood by writing them on the red figures before hanging them up.

In earlier times these lucky charms were thought to ward off demons and evil spirits, but today they are more likely to be acting as protection against disease or, for students, poor exam results. For women they are supposed to protect against infertility, painful childbirth and marriage difficulties. Some women even buy red underclothes called *saru-mata*, said to be imitations of the red rumps of female monkeys on heat, to encourage pregnancy.

2 Tribal Monkeys: Myths and Superstitions

Tribal societies, especially in tropical Africa, frequently create monkey masks or figurines and use them in a variety of ceremonies, dances and rituals. In many tribes the wild monkeys that are seen scampering about high up in the trees are admired for their intelligence and quick-wittedness. In tribal rituals, the character of the monkey is usually that of a wild, untamed spirit, sometimes comical, sometimes mildly threatening, sometimes positively sinister and dangerous. Some monkey images are used in initiation rites, some in harvest ceremonies, some in rituals to protect the tribes from evil spirits, and some in funeral or death ceremonies. In certain tribes, instead of making monkey carvings, the skulls of the animal themselves are employed in witchcraft.

DOGON TRIBE: AFRICA

The Dogon tribe are cliff-dwellers who live in southeast Mali. Masked dancing is of special importance to them and the masks are believed to possess a life force of their own. The restrained behaviour of a typical Dogon tribesman contrasts strongly with the personality of the monkey portrayed in ceremonies by certain of these masked performers. For the Dogon, in ritual dances the monkey represents dangerous, uncivilized, antisocial behaviour.

A white monkey
Dogon dance
mask with a
stylized monkey
figure perched
on top of
the head.

There are three kinds of monkey mask in Dogon society, distinguished not by their design but by their colour. The black monkey is called Dege, the white monkey is Omono and the red is Ko. The black monkey is known as the male villain of the bush, an animal that preys on the crops and is renowned for his gluttony, unpredictability and general wickedness. Worn as a mask, it provides the anti-aesthetic, anti-humanistic reversal of correct human behaviour. It also represents the dark forces of sorcery that are greatly feared by the tribesmen.

When the dancer wearing the black monkey mask is dancing in a ceremony he hears the words: 'Ugly male of the bush sitting at the top of a tall tree. Your stomach full of fruit all eyes are on you . . . the drum plays for you.'

The white and red monkeys do not seem to be much better than the black: in dances they symbolize 'improper behaviour, such as thievery or laziness'.

BAULE TRIBE: AFRICA

Monkey figures play an important role in the art of the Baule tribe in the Ivory Coast region of West Africa. Their *Mbra* or *Gbekre* monkey figures are among the most powerful and frightening of all their sculptural works, so much so that they have to be kept secret and hidden under a shelter or in the bush because it is thought that they might be dangerous to women. When they are brought out they are used by the tribal trance diviners of the men's associations for protection against sorcerers. They are especially prominent during initiation ceremonies. They are also used in agrarian rites when, if properly honoured, they will grant fruitful harvests and successful hunts.

An old example of Baule monkey sculptures.

Old examples of these monkey sculptures are often found to have encrusted surfaces, due to the sacrificial blood offerings that have been poured over them as libations during tribal rituals, and they are thought to feed on these libations. So important are these monkey sculptures that they are believed to embody the animal part of the human spirit. The Baule believe that this element in the make-up of the human spirit exists in every person and that it resides in the bush. The carved figures sometimes incorporate a real monkey skull in their design to give it a more powerful impact. The monkey is usually shown holding in its paws a small bowl that contained an egg during the divination rituals.

In addition to the small, portable carvings, there are some large, sinister, life-sized figures made specially to guard a particular place or even a whole village.

One of the *Mbra* or *Gbekre* monkey figures of the Baule tribe.

Some neighbouring tribes in the Ivory Coast region, like the Dan, have a more light-hearted approach towards monkey images. For them the wearing of a *Kaogle* monkey mask during ceremonies is intended to add a comic touch to the proceedings, with the wearer playing the role of a village clown.

AZTECS: CENTRAL AMERICA

In the Pre-Columbian art of Central America, the monkey was portrayed in a more appealing manner than among African tribes. It was associated with dance, art, beauty, music, song, harmony, happiness, games and fun – in other words, the playful monkey.

For the Aztecs the monkey god was Ozomatli, the companion spirit and servant of the god Xochipilli, the deity of music and dance. In paintings it is depicted dressed in *malinalli* herbs and with white, oval earrings with pointed ends. These earrings are said to be based on the conch shell. Sometimes the whole monkey is shown, sometimes only its head, with its tongue sticking out.

The Aztecs' monkey god Ozomatli.

It has been claimed that it was the Central American monkeys who introduced mankind to the joys of eating chocolate. Apparently, the Aztecs noticed that monkeys liked to eat the sweet pulp concealed within the pods of the cacao plant. The animals swallowed the pulp but spat out the beans. The Aztecs followed suit, in this way discovering chocolate, thanks to the monkeys. For these people, chocolate became more than just a food: it was looked upon with awe as a divine gift and a source of power.

MAYANS: CENTRAL AMERICA

If the Aztecs special monkey deity, Ozomatli, was based on a spider monkey, the Mayans' equivalent, Batz, was taken from its close relative, the howler monkey. Howlers were depicted on

The Mayans' special monkey deity, Batz.

Classic Mayan vases in the act of writing books and carving heads. This suggests that they were the patrons of the artisans, especially the scribes and the sculptors. There is also one instance, at the ancient site of Copan, where two large monkey statues show them as musicians, shaking rattles.

KUNA INDIANS: CENTRAL AMERICA

On the *molas* made by the Kuna Indians of Panama the Tree of Life is shown with its branches full of tiny monkeys.

Sadly, the surviving native cultures of the New World rarely create works of art today that depict monkeys. In the depths of the Amazon, the few remaining isolated tribal groups occasionally keep young monkeys as pets, but their art is confined largely to their own body decoration.

There is one culture, however, that is an exception to this rule and that still depicts monkeys in their art. The Kuna Indians of Panama, living on an archipelago of small islands off the northern coast, continue to produce a tribal art form that is bravely resisting modernization. The Kuna women make decorative panels called *molas* that they wear as part of their traditional costume. Some of these *molas* are abstract but others display pictorial images including a variety of animal forms. A favourite theme is the 'Tree of Life' because it plays such a central role in their belief system. It is thought that when the sun-god mated with the earth-mother she gave birth to all forms of nature attached to an enormous tree. The Tree of Life is therefore like a vast umbilical cord connected to all the animals, plants and humans that populate the surface of the earth.

Sometimes the Tree of Life is shown with its branches full of animals, and a favourite example of this is the tree in which a horde of tiny monkeys seem to occupy every inch of space. In one *mola* there are no fewer than 32 monkeys visible.

It is difficult to identify the precise species of monkey that appears in Kuna *molas* because they are always so highly stylized. Although all real monkeys have flat faces, the Kuna artists perversely give them sharply pointed beaks, like birds. They sometimes do the same with human figures because, apparently, a pointed nose is looked upon as a mark of beauty. The Kuna monkeys can, however, be identified as such by their curled, prehensile tails.

3 Monkeys Despised

In the earlier centuries of the Western world, before Charles Darwin persuaded people to respect monkeys as our close relations, they were generally looked down on as evil, wicked creatures, or as obscene hairy brutes, or the epitome of foolishness, motivated by the outlandish presumption that they can pass themselves off as human beings. Indeed, it is true to say that in the past they have suffered more from mankind's exaggerated sense of his own superiority that any other kind of animal.

THE ANCIENT WORLD: GREECE AND ROME

The ancient Greeks were particularly offended by the monkey's lack of smoothly rounded buttocks – a feature acquired by the human species during the course of evolution as a result of switching to upright walking. The lean-bottomed monkeys, with their ischial callosities – tough patches of hardened skin on which they sit – were attacked as being both unsightly and immodest. To make matters worse, in many species, the female monkey's rear-end periodically becomes even more conspicuous, being adorned with a large, raw-looking sexual swelling.[1]

Because monkeys seemed so ugly to human observers, the question was asked, 'Could it be that an ugly body houses an ugly mind?' Sadly for the monkey, the early philosophers' answer was

'Yes!' and it soon became widely believed that if the monkey was physically repulsive it must follow that it was also morally vile.

This concept of the monkey as an evil being has a long history. Writing in the seventh century BC, the Greek poet Simonides identifies the very worst kind of woman as descending from the monkey:

> In appearance most ugly; when such a woman shows herself in the street, people laugh at her. She is short in the neck, hardly moves, has no buttocks, is withered of limb; unhappy a man who embraces such a pest. And she knows all the intrigues and tricks like a monkey, nor does she ever care to laugh. Nor will she do a good turn to anyone, but it is her aim which she plans every day how she may do him the greatest injury.

In ancient Rome the monkey was used as a token of humiliation in the punishment of individuals who had killed their fathers. The culprit was whipped, then sewn up in a sack with a monkey and various other animals and thrown in the Tiber or the sea to drown. The monkey was included in this terrible punishment because, as an ugly caricature of man, it was a suitable companion for those who had murdered their own flesh and blood.

As sinners, monkeys became notorious for their outbursts of violent anger and their savage attacks on humans. These attacks were undoubtedly genuine, not because the animals were by nature unduly aggressive, but simply because of the brutal way in which captive specimens were usually treated by their ignorant captors.

Monkeys were also considered useless as domesticated animals. Plutarch said that a monkey could not guard the house like a dog, or work like a horse or an ox, therefore its only use was for it to be made a sport of and an object of laughter.

The monkey's supposedly disastrous desire to imitate humans was the basis for an anecdote of Aelian's in which a monkey, having seen the way in which a nurse bathed a baby, then tried to copy her actions, placing a baby in boiling water and killing it. And there is an old tale in which the pet monkey of a sleeping king sees a fly alight on his master's chest, searches for a dagger and tries to stab the fly, only killing his master in the process.

The monkey's reputation for imitating people, probably fostered by early displays of performing monkeys that were trained to mimic human actions, was used as the basis for the idea that the animal was trying to convince people that he really was one of them. This led to him being labelled as the prototype of the imposter, the fraud and the trickster. In particular he became identified as representing the person of lowly origin who pretends to a high position and gave rise to the old proverb: 'An ape's an ape, a varlet's a varlet, though they be clad in silk or scarlet.' As early as the fourth century, the Roman poet Claudian, attacking an elderly consul, described him as a monkey dressed in silk.

The advent of Christianity saw the reputation of the monkey sink even lower. From the fall of the Roman empire until the late Middle Ages the official view of the Christian Church was that the monkey was a diabolical beast.[2] In the fourth century, when early Christian zealots were eagerly setting about the destruction of Egyptian idols in Alexandria, their leader ordered that one statue should be preserved as a monument to heathen depravity. Needless to say, that statue was one of a sacred baboon. The monkey-god of the ancient Egyptians had, in one powerful gesture, become the monkey-devil of Christianity. The Devil himself became known as Simia Dei or God's Monkey.

Monkeys appeared in most of the medieval bestiaries, where five kinds were identified. There was the ape, the name then given to the Barbary macaque; the monkey, which was described as the same as the ape except that it had a long tail; the baboon from Ethiopia; the Sphinx, another kind of ape; and the satyr, also from Ethiopia.

The first of these, the ape, was said to be cheerful when the moon was new and sad when it waned. When the mother ape had twins she was reputed to love one and hate the other. As a sign of her stupidity, it was claimed that if she were chased by a hunter, she would clasp to her chest the twin she loved and let the one she hated cling to her back. Then, if the hunter came close, she would drop the one she loved, and run off with the one she hated still clinging to her back. This is the origin of the modern phrase 'having a monkey on your back'.

Anatomically, the ape did not fare well in the hands of these early bestiary writers. It is clear that primates were too close to humans for comfort and had to be belittled as much as possible, to keep them in their place. To quote one author, writing between 1220 and 1250: 'If the whole of the ape is hateful, his backside is even more horrible and disgusting . . . their faces are horrible, with folds, like a disgusting pair of bellows.'[3] A little earlier, in 1210, a French bestiary writer stated bluntly that 'there is nothing I can liken to the ape for it is all bad'.[4]

Apes were said to be fond of imitating humans and the best way to catch one was for the trapper to sit down and keep taking off and putting on his boot. Then he went away, leaving the boot tethered to a tree. The ape, unable to resist copying the trapper, would then approach and put the boot on, when it was easy to capture.

Three hunters attacking a family of monkeys, from a mid-13th century English Bestiary, with one monkey already shot in the head by an arrow.

In this scene from a late 12th-century English Bestiary the illustrator shows us a frightened female monkey carrying twins, being hunted by an archer.

Baboons, it was said, were great leapers, savage biters and impossible to tame. Sphinxes, on the other hand, with their shaggy upper arms, could be taught to forget their wild ways. Satyrs, with hairy bodies, beards, broad tails and almost pleasing faces, had strange, restless gestures and were easy to catch. Kept captive, however, they quickly died, for they could only thrive under their native Ethiopian sky. They were symbols of debauchery.

From these quaint descriptions it is clear that, in thirteenth-century Europe, monkeys were little known and less understood. The overall impression is that the pious bestiary makers found them profoundly unpleasant and wished to give them the worst possible image.

EMBLEM BOOKS: 16TH AND 17TH CENTURIES

In the emblem books of the sixteenth and seventeenth centuries, monkeys rarely figured, but when they did, they appeared as shameful and disgusting. It was their rear ends that caused so much embarrassment, with the naked red swellings of the females rising and falling with their sexual cycles in an inescapable manner. When seen from below, as when a monkey climbed up higher than the human eye-line, this 'disfigurement' was even more conspicuous. This led to an amusing epigram in Jacob Cats's book of emblems of 1632:

The higher one climbs
The more one shows
One's shameful parts

These words accompanied an etching showing a captive monkey tethered to a vertical pole. The monkey has clambered

A monkey climbs to the top of a pole and reveals its rump in an emblem book of 1632.

to the top of the pole and, below it, startled human figures point in outrage and disbelief at its revolting rump.[5]

The moral of this epigram, that the higher a person climbs up the social ladder, the more he or she will display the shameful aspects of their personality, has a double meaning for us today. First, it implies that those who manage to struggle to the top of the social pile must privately be pretty vicious, even if publicly they appear as philanthropic do-gooders. Whatever they may say, their high status automatically marks them out as shamefully ruthless, and the higher they go, the more shameful they get. Second, in today's intrusive world of paparazzi, gossip magazines, kiss-and-tell stories and the cult of overinflated celebrity, there is an even more direct way in which this old epigram can find its mark. As every A-list celebrity knows all too well, the moment you reach the pinnacle of modern society, instead of being protected from exposure, you are much more vulnerable to it. If you expose a nipple, flash a buttock or have your toes sucked, you become the focus of a media frenzy. If you are at the bottom of the social ladder, nobody cares. The monkey-up-the-pole epigram fits perfectly here – even more than it did when first published.

Monkeys were such a rarity in Europe that their role as deeply wicked and evil beings did not last. As the centuries passed, they were still despised, but in a gentler way. Now they became a popular device in humorous art and literature, where they were employed as caricatures of ridiculed humans. If you wanted to poke fun at artists, politicians, priests, aristocrats, doctors, teachers or any other branch of civilized society, you portrayed these august beings, not as humans, but as monkeys dressed as humans. The sinful monkey had become the foolish monkey.

The monkey artist first appeared in the seventeenth century. Portrait artists who flattered their subjects by making them look more attractive than they were in life were looked on as cunning liars who should be despised for not having the courage to tell the truth about the appearance of their sitters. In the 1790s, Francisco Goya, in an etching from his *Los Caprichos* series, satirized this idea by showing a monkey portraying an ungainly donkey as a distinguished-looking horse. The pompous ass becomes transformed into the noble horse wearing a curly wig.

Also in the eighteenth century, the French artist Jean-Baptiste Chardin showed a monkey hard at work on an important canvas. The animal is setting out to paint a still-life, the centrepiece of which is an antique statue. The message Chardin intends here is that the painter is no more than a mimic, or monkey, if he insists on copying the work of other artists rather than taking his inspiration directly from nature. The painting was so popular that Chardin painted it several times to keep up with demand.

Francisco Goya's monkey portrays a donkey as a horse, from the *Los Caprichos* series of etchings of 1799.

In the early nineteenth century J. J. Grandville had great fun mocking two opposing schools of art. The Academic School led by Ingres is depicted as a baboon blindly tracing the outline of a human leg from a drawing signed 'Raphael'. The point is driven home by the fact that the baboon is literally blindfolded and is sitting astride a wooden horse with Raphael's face. Stretched out behind him in a series of smaller and smaller replicas are his pupils all doing the same. In other words, Ingres is shown as a foolish monkey because he slavishly copies the work of earlier masters

Jean-Baptiste Chardin, *The Monkey Painter*, c. 1739–40, oil on canvas.

– an ignoble mimic. The Romantic School, led by Delacroix, is depicted as a trio of monkeys painting with wanton abandon. One paints with his tail, another with his foot. In other words, Delacroix and the Romantics care nothing for technique, merely striking poses and lazily producing emotional mediocrity.

In 1827 the British animal artist Edwin Landseer entered the world of monkey satire with his painting *The Monkey Who had Seen the World*. It shows a local monkey made good, dressed as a Regency buck, proudly standing on his hind legs while surrounded by envious stay-at-home monkeys, naked and squatting miserably on the ground. The inescapable message in this work is that the artist prefers the showy success to the dowdy failure. Had he favoured happy villagers over pretentious snobs, the portrayals would have been quite different. Significantly, the successful monkey is portrayed as almost human, while the miserable stay-at-homes are depicted in a naturalistic way, as pure monkeys. This can be seen as suggesting an additional message. The artist seems to be saying both that human stay-at-homes are inferior to human go-getters, and that monkeys are inferior to men.

Edwin Landseer, *The Monkey Who Had Seen the World*, 1827, oil on canvas.

Using monkeys satirically was popular in both the eighteenth and the nineteenth centuries. The first sign of objection to this approach came in the famous Darwin debate at Oxford in 1860. It was then that Soapy Sam, the notorious Bishop Wilberforce of Oxford, asked his fatal question of Darwin's champion, Thomas Henry Huxley, as to whether 'it was it through his grandfather or his grandmother that he claimed his descent from a monkey?' When Huxley replied that 'he would not be ashamed to have a monkey for his ancestor, but he would be ashamed to be connected with a man who used his great gifts to obscure the truth', he not only won the debate, but also placed a humble monkey above a devious human. This elevated the monkey to an entirely new level in human thought and marked the end of centuries of abuse. The despised monkey was about to fade into history.

A blindfolded baboon traces an outline from a drawing signed 'Raphael' in J. J. Grandville's cartoon of art training in Ingres' Academic School.

The Romantic School led by Delacroix in Grandville's cartoon.

4 Lustful Monkeys

There is one special feature of the 'unpleasant' monkey that demands closer examination and this is its imagined super-virility. Since ancient times there have been wild rumours of monkeys coupling with humans, sometimes brutally raping them and sometimes enjoying the favours of willing partners.[1]

The great irony of these imagined debaucheries is that, in real life, the sexual behaviour of monkeys is far from being excessive. In the wild, the typical monkey mating act lasts for an average of only eight seconds. So how did the monkey acquire the reputation of being so lewd and lustful?

There are several answers. The first is that the monkey has so often been seen as the animalistic face of humanity. It has gained the image of being the equivalent of human beings with all of their civilized veneer stripped away, leaving only the base instincts of the jungle. This makes them perfect candidates to act as symbols of lechery. Second, the first important monkey companion – the sacred baboon of ancient Egypt – was notorious for its spectacular penis, always conspicuously displayed in statues of the crouching baboon Thoth. Add to this the fact that the sexual parts of live monkeys – both male and female – are highly conspicuous and that they make no attempt to hide them, or to seek privacy for mating, as humans do, and you have a good starting point for the myth of the rapist monkey or the monkey lover.

The sacred baboon of ancient Egypt was notorious for its spectacular and highly conspicuous penis.

This legend gained momentum from one of the tales in the Arabian classic, *The Thousand Nights and a Night.* This huge collection of stories started life in Asia in the third century and first appeared in Arabic in the ninth. It went through many stages of development after that, mostly from oral repetition, so it is hard to date any one particular story, but it is safe to say that they are all very early in their origins.[2]

In the story of 'The King's Daughter and the Ape', the ape in question is almost certainly a baboon. The heroine of the story, if heroine is the appropriate word, is a sultan's daughter who loses her virginity to a black slave. In his company she becomes so addicted to lovemaking that she gradually becomes insatiable and he can no longer satisfy her needs. She complains about this to a female servant who tells her that a baboon is her only hope, since they too are insatiable. One day she catches sight of a baboon being led down the street below and signals to him with her eyes.

The animal understands and promptly climbs the wall and enters her chambers. She hides him there and in the days that follow enjoys his almost non-stop sexual attentions. Her father hears about this and decides his daughter must die. To escape him she flees to Cairo with her indispensible baboon. Seeing her worn appearance, a young man becomes so curious about her that he follows her and spies on her in her bedroom. He is astonished to see her enjoying repeated and passionate lovemaking with her baboon, lovemaking so exhausting that she eventually swoons right away. At this point the young man can stand it no longer, rushes in and slays the baboon. The sultan's daughter is woken by this and, when she sees her lover lying dead, she 'shrieks such a

In the Arabian Nights story of 'The King's Daughter and the Ape', a sultan's daughter enjoys all too well the company of a large monkey.

shriek that her soul near flees her body'. The young man does his best to take over the sexual duties of the baboon, but he simply cannot keep up with the girl's demands. He consults a wise old woman who performs a secret ritual and removes a black worm and a yellow worm from the girl's body, explaining that the black worm was implanted by the black slave and the yellow one by the baboon. After their removal the girl's nymphomania is finally cured.

The unusual feature of this story is the girl's distress at the loss of her monkey partner. Most of the early tales of sex-mad monkeys see them as brutal rapists, savagely attacking women whenever they get the chance. However, this baboon is a not a hated violator but an athletic lover.

Much later, in Voltaire's *Candide* (1759), there is an echo of this tale when Candide, exploring the Amazon forests, hears faint female cries. He is unable to tell whether these are cries of joy or grief, so he investigates. He discovers that they are coming from two naked girls who are running away from two monkeys. He is horrified to see that the monkeys are biting the girls' buttocks, so he takes up a gun and shoots the animals dead. He is convinced that he has 'rescued these two poor creatures from a grave peril', but is then astonished to see that the girls are now 'tenderly kissing the two monkeys, shedding tears on their bodies and filling the air with the most piteous cries'. Comically, Candide interprets this behaviour on the part of the girls as an extraordinary example of 'Christian charity'. But his servant puts him straight and suggests that they should flee for their safety as soon as possible.

The key similarity between these two tales, centuries apart, are the moments when the females involved reveal that they adore their monkey lovers and are distraught at losing them. This puts a new twist on the 'despised monkey', for here it is only the men in the stories who hate the monkeys and look upon them as brutal lechers. For the women, they are far from despised, and this puts them into a special category. The moral of these two stories seems to be that men do not put enough of their animal passion into their relations with women. The role of the monkeys here is a reminder of their folly in this respect.

With rapist monkeys, the message is completely different. Here mankind is noble and nature is savage. If a woman allows herself to be snatched away by forces of natures she will be debauched. One of the earliest references to this is in the fourth century BC when the Greek general and statesman Timotheus asserts that monkeys in general are brutal and licentious. Then, in the second-century writings of the Greek military author Aelian there is the claim that old male baboons are lascivious and will attack women and children.

Although there was never any direct evidence of a wild monkey raping a woman, this tall tale became firmly embedded in European folklore and repeatedly resurfaced. In the sixteenth century, for example, it is seriously reported that the baboon 'loves women and children . . . and will try openly to cohabit with the latter whenever it escapes its fetters'.

In legends where humans and monkeys consummated their relationships there were often children of these unions. These offspring were usually described as hybrid monsters, but none were ever available for scientific study. The moral of the story is changing again. Now it is 'mate with your own kind or you are in trouble'. The monkeys in these cases are being employed as symbols of inter-racial connections that, in earlier days, were considered so unacceptable.

Before leaving the lustful monkeys, it is worth asking whether there are any small truths hidden in the outlandish yarns that have been told for so many centuries. Is it all make-believe, or could something have connected across the genetic divide between

Les deux égarés entendirent quelques petits cris qui paraissaient poussés par des femmes.

Candide, Ch. XVI.

An illustration of *c.* 1800 for Voltaire's *Candide* (1759), in which the hero kills the girls' monkey lovers.

human and monkey. The most likely answer is that nothing sexual has ever happened between a wild monkey and a human being, either male or female. Pet monkeys, however, are another matter. If a monkey is hand-reared from birth by a human carer, it is entirely possible that, when the monkey becomes mature, it may direct some sexual interest towards the body of its human companion, just as a pet dog will hump its owner's leg. However, the monkey penis is never as large as the human organ and, as mentioned earlier, it only takes a male monkey eight seconds to reach ejaculation. So, even if there has been an occasional, real monkey lover, its performance will inevitably have been hugely disappointing.

5 Monkeys Enjoyed

Human beings have enjoyed the company of monkeys for centuries. Their intelligence and playfulness have appealed to those pet-keepers who have sought an animal companion that is more exotic than the usual cats and dogs. Inevitably, their ability to leap with great agility, and therefore cause domestic havoc, has limited their acceptance as household pets, but their expressive faces and their ability to manipulate small objects in a human manner have given them a special appeal. For the more adventurous pet-keeper, they have been a challenge worth accepting.

In Tudor England, monkeys were favoured pets of the royal courts. They were difficult to obtain and their ownership therefore became a display of high status. Portraits of Tudor monarchs reveal that Elizabeth I, Catherine of Aragon and Edward VI all kept pet monkeys. These animals not only played the role of court jesters, but were also said to have been used in the training of dogs for bear and bull-baiting, although it is not clear how this would have been achieved.

Painted in 1531, the miniature of Henry VIII's first wife, Catherine of Aragon, with her pet capuchin monkey, shows the animal reaching out for the crucifix that the Queen is

Catherine of Aragon, 1531; her pet capuchin monkey touches the crucifix.

wearing. It seems likely that this gesture reflects no more than the monkey's natural curiosity, but those art historians who see symbols in every detail of early paintings have interpreted the monkey's action as a veiled attack on either her husband, Henry, or the new love of his life, Anne Boleyn, who would replace Catherine as queen. To support their theory, they point out that in an earlier version of the painting, dating from 1525, there is no crucifix. It only appears in the 1531 miniature, by which time her marriage was in serious trouble, with Henry determined to get a divorce even if he had to split from the Catholic Church.

As an attack on Henry, the monkey's gesture is seen as symbolizing Henry fiddling with the rules of the Catholic Church in an attempt to get his divorce. As an attack on Anne Boleyn it is said to be a hidden insult that likens Anne to a meddling monkey.

In addition to keeping monkeys to show off at court, royalty sometimes used them to alleviate the loneliness of their elevated position. Princesses, often starved of close parental affection, found an emotional outlet in keeping pets. There is a report that, when young, Princess Elizabeth, who would later become Elizabeth I, tried to teach her pet monkey to play tennis.

Another Elizabeth, James I's daughter, Elizabeth of Bohemia, had so many pets during her isolated childhood that it was said: 'Of little dogs and monkeys, she hath no great want, having sixteen or seventeen in her own train.' When she married in 1612, her husband created an 'English Wing' for her at Heidelberg Castle, complete with its own monkey-house. She later became notorious for favouring her pets above her offspring and her daughter claimed that her mother preferred 'the sight of her monkeys and dogs to that of her children'.

Also in the seventeenth century, a famous pet monkey belonged to Prince Rupert of the Rhine, a nephew of Charles I. A satirical tract about this animal was published in 1642, with the delightful title of *The Humerous Tricks and Conceits of Prince Roberts Malignant She-Monkey, discovered to the world before her marriage. Also the manner of her marriage to a Cavalier and how within three dayes space, she called him Cuckold to his face.* The cover picture of this tract shows the monkey smoking a clay pipe and holding hands with her cavalier.

A little earlier, at the very start of the seventeenth century, there is a bizarre story about a pet monkey that snatched a sleeping baby from its cradle and scampered up on to flat roof of the house where it lived. When it was noticed up there playing with the infant, the household panicked and began placing beds and blankets on the ground below to break the baby's fall if the monkey dropped it. It was far too careful for that, however, and held tight to its prize until, of its own accord, it came back down to the ground. The baby was rescued, safe and sound, and grew up to

Even isolated Amazonian tribes, like the Awa, are known to keep monkeys as pets.

An anonymous satirical tract of 1642 concerning a famous pet monkey belonging to Prince Rupert of the Rhine.

THE   9

HUMEROUS
TRICKS AND CONCEITS OF
Prince *Roberts* Malignant She-Monkey, dif-
covered to the world before her marriage.

Alfo the manner of her marriage to a **Cavaleer and how**
within three dayes fpace, fhe called him Cuckold to his face.

OutCuckold

164 London, printed for *T. Cornifh.* March. 15

become the infamous Oliver Cromwell. Had the monkey been a little less careful, England might have been spared its Civil War.

In eighteenth-century Russia, Catherine the Great's final lover, the ambitious young Prince Zubov, who was 40 years her junior, held such power over Russia that royal courtiers found it hard to gain close contact with him and had to resort to currying favour with his pet monkey in the hope that this would stand them in good stead. Zubov was highly amused when the monkey would then jump on their shoulders and steal their wigs, leaving them in a state of gross courtly embarrassment.

It was said of the eccentric second Baron Rothschild that, in the nineteenth century, he regularly shared his table at his Buckinghamshire mansion, Waddesdon Manor, with his pet monkeys and on one occasion gave a special party 'with 12 dressed monkeys'. Legend has it that this was an important political dinner in honour of Lord Salisbury and that when the twelve guests were seated at the table, they were surprised to see that each had an empty chair beside them. Then, just before the meal began, twelve immaculately dressed monkeys are reputed to have walked in and sat down in the empty seats.

In the twentieth century the more eccentric of the great celebrities have – with a little help from their servants – kept the occasional pet monkey. Mae West had a number of them in the 1930s, rearing them as her children. One of them, called Boogie, was the cause of an amusing misunderstanding. Mae West's famous ad lib to her maid, 'Beulah, peel me a grape', was interpreted as a grotesque demand by an impossible diva. In reality, she was asking her maid to prepare a titbit, not for herself, but for Boogie, who was the true diva, and refused to eat a grape unless it was pre-peeled for her.

Mae West with her pet monkey Boogie.

An American
newspaper
advertisement
of the 1950s
offering monkeys
for sale now
seems strangely
unpleasant.

Hollywood has often made use of the presence of a pet monkey to liven up a scene and, in the popular film series *Pirates of the Caribbean*, instead of having the traditional parrot on his shoulder, Captain Hector Barbossa has a pet monkey called Jack. Although supposedly male, it is in reality a more amenable female called Chiquita. As its acting role in the film requires high intelligence, it is not surprising to discover that Chiquita is a capuchin. 'The monkey actually is the smartest person in the film', says the actor Geoffrey Rush, who plays Barbossa.

In modern times, the keeping of monkeys at home as domestic pets has gradually fallen out of favour. Several countries, including Holland, Israel, Mexico and India, have already banned the practice. The same is true of nineteen states in the USA (California, Colorado, Connecticut, Georgia, Kentucky, Louisiana, Maine, Maryland, Massachusetts, Minnesota, New Hampshire,

New Jersey, New Mexico, New York, Pennsylvania, Rhode Island, Utah, Vermont and Wyoming). Congress is considering the Captive Primate Safety Act that would prohibit interstate commerce in pet monkeys. In January 2012 the British parliament debated the advisability of introducing a similar ban in the United Kingdom. The reason given for introducing this restriction was that 'monkeys suffer by being kept as household pets'. This is often true and it could have been added that their owners frequently suffer too.

There are several reasons why, despite their enormous appeal, monkeys do not make good pets. They are largely tropical animals and, unlike cats and dogs, do not take well to a colder climate. This means they require specially heated accommodation that is often not available to them. The smaller species of monkeys are rather delicate and, because they are biologically close to their owners, can easily pick up human infections. They can also transmit some of their own diseases to humans. Also, although the bigger ones may be hugely appealing when young, they are usually

This tiny pet monkey is a sad sight, condemned to a life of unnatural restraint. Despite their enormous appeal, monkeys do not make good pets.

The official view today is that 'Keeping monkeys as pets threatens public health and safety as well as animal welfare'. Despite this, TV is still unable to resist the storyline appeal of a pet capuchin.

dangerous when they become adults, especially in their reactions to strangers. The damage that can be done by the bite of a large monkey can easily be underestimated.

In addition, monkeys do not take kindly to life in a small cage. They are by nature much too athletic to be confined in restricted quarters. And when let loose they can quickly cause havoc inside the home or panic when they escape from it. Finally, unlike dogs and cats, it is difficult, if not impossible, to toilet-train them.

If, despite all these shortcomings, and with the law permitting, a pet-keeper is determined to own a monkey, then there is really only one kind that worth considering: the New World capuchin. These are not only the most intelligent of all monkeys, but also the most adaptable. It is no accident that they were the favourite companions of street performers in earlier centuries or of professional animal trainers in modern times.

Even with the patient and amenable capuchins, however, there are loud voices being raised against the idea of keeping them as pets. Lynn Cuny, the founder of a wildlife rescue centre in America, who has to care for a large number of ex-pet capuchins whose owners could not longer cope, is highly critical, and Beth Preiss, a specialist in captive wildlife with the Humane Society of the United States, has a blunt, uncompromising message for would-be monkey pet-owners:

> Keeping monkeys as pets threatens public health and safety as well as animal welfare. They can attack, they can spread disease and the average pet owner cannot meet their needs in captivity.

It is fair to say that this statement succinctly sums up the modern Western attitude to pet monkeys. As the twenty-first century wears on, we are likely to see more and more legislation introduced to limit this activity which, although it may offer the most expert pet-keepers many otherwise unobtainable insights into the behaviour and personality of primates, brings with it a barrel-load of problems.

MONKEYS AS PERFORMERS

Monkey performers have been entertaining the public for centuries and it is a sad fact that some species, especially the capuchins and the smaller macaques, have been so amenable to training by showmen that they have been coerced into acting in a variety of unnatural ways. Sometimes the performance has involved a monkey, dressed as a clown, imitating some kind of human activity. At other times, it was simply enough for the animal to sit in its fancy human costume and look like a comically small man.

In seventeenth-century London, performing monkeys were a regular form of entertainment at the annual Bartholomew Fair. In

A street performance in India, earning the monkey's trainer a modest living.

his diary entry for 31 August 1661, Samuel Pepys recorded: 'I back again to the fair all alone . . . seeing the monkeys dance, which was much to see, when they could be brought to do so.' Two years later, Pepys was back again and on 4 September 1663, commented:

> Thence . . . to Bartholomew Fayre, where I have no mind to go without my wife . . . and so carried her by coach to the fayre, and showed her the monkeys dancing on the ropes, which was strange, but such dirty sport that I was not pleased with it.

Three days later he returned

> to Bartholomew Fayre, where I met with Mr Pickering, and he and I to see the monkeys at the Dutch house, which is far beyond the other that my wife and I saw the other day; and thence to see the dancing on the ropes, which was very poor and tedious.

In the following century, monkey performances seem to have improved. A Signor Spinacuti entertained the French king and his court with a trained monkey called 'Le Chevalier des Singes'. This animal's act included 'dancing and tumbling on the slack and tight rope; balancing a chandelier, a hoop and a tobacco-pipe on the tip of his nose and chin, and making a melodramatic exit in a shower of fireworks'. In 1767, he also appeared at Sadler's Wells Theatre in London, where his performance was described as 'walking and dancing on the tightrope with a pole and on the wire with and without a pole, vaulting on the slack rope, and turning the Catherine Wheel'.

Perhaps the best-remembered example of a performing simian is the barrel-organ monkey of the nineteenth century. The barrel

In the 18th century, Signor Spinacuti's performing monkey, 'Le Chevalier des Singes', appeared at Sadler's Wells Theatre, London, where he walked the tightrope.

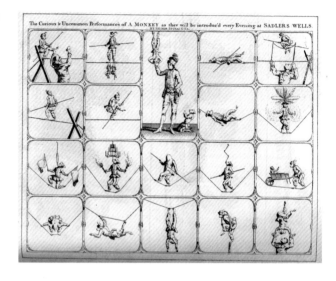

The Curious & Uncommon Performances of A MONKEY as they will be introduce'd every Evening at SADLERS WELLS BY SIGNOR SPINACUTI

organ was a portable instrument that was operated by turning a handle and played simple tunes as a way of earning coins for street buskers. In order to attract attention, the organ-grinder was often accompanied by a costumed capuchin monkey that was trained to collect the coins. People were more likely to give money if they were faced with the novelty of handing their coins to a begging monkey and this form of street entertainment became so successful that at one time there were no fewer than 1,500 organ-grinders on the streets of New York. In London, Charles Dickens complained that he could 'not write for more than half an hour without being disturbed by the most excruciating sounds imaginable, coming in from barrel organs on the street'. When music copyright laws were introduced at the start of the twentieth century, barrel organs soon vanished, and with them their pathetic little monkeys.

In the 1930s a new kind of monkey performer appeared on the scene – the monkey jockey. Once again it was the intelligent,

Best-remembered of all performing simians is the barrel-organ monkey of the 19th century, who was trained to collect the coins.

The Organ Grinder. No. 1

Overpeck HAMILTON, O.

cooperative capuchin who suffered the indignity of being dressed up, this time as a joke version of a human jockey on the back of a racing greyhound. Teams of capuchins were trained to compete in greyhound races in the United States, Mexico, China and Australia between 1930 and the late 1950s, after which the craze eventually died out.

At the Orange Park greyhound track in Florida it was the eleventh race of the day that was the special 'monkey race'. An eyewitness reported:

> The monkeys paraded onto the track for their race . . . They each wore oilskin capes over their silk riding suits and . . . the monkeys appear to take especial pleasure if their greyhound wins and often become angry, striking their dog if he loses. The race drew the fans from the covered grandstand into the rain to get a better glimpse.

In Australia, the monkeys even had to endure jump races, clinging on tightly as their canine mounts leapt over hurdles and water-jumps. Luckily for these monkeys, clinging onto the back of a large animal had a natural echo of what they must have experienced on the backs of their mothers when they were infants in the wild.

Recently there has been a resurgence of interest in monkey jockeys. They are now employed in a performance called The Banana Derby that tours American fairs and festivals, but the racing is less serious. Now they are saddled on the backs of various cross-breed dogs and the event is less demanding than the original greyhound racing. Even so, all such animal entertainments are now on the receiving end of severe criticism from animal welfare organizations. PETA (People for the Ethical Treatment of Animals) condemns them all, saying:

Games, rides, and contests that use animals are anything but 'fun and games' for the unwilling animal participants. These cruel events are often part of fundraisers and fairs. The animals are carted from town to town, and they live in a state of discomfort, frustration, depression and anxiety.

This attitude is growing in the West today, where public opinion has been shifting further and further away from animal displays in circuses and sideshows. These are now widely seen as relics of an ignorant past, when people did not understand the true nature of environmental needs of animals. In the East, however, this shift has barely begun. There, monkey entertainers do still exist on the streets and on stages, wearily plying their trade. Street monkeys are common, for example, in Indonesia. In the heart of the city of Jakarta, on the island of Java, one of the strangest of all monkey presentations can be found. What makes these costumed macaques so bizarre are the human masks that they are made to wear, giving them the look of some small alien beings. Once caught, these animals are kept in a monkey-training

Even today, street monkeys are common in Indonesia where, in the heart of the city of Jakarta, costumed macaques wear human masks, giving them a bizarre appearance.

On the island of Ko Samui in Thailand, there is a Monkey Theatre where pigtailed macaques entertain paying audiences.

village until they are ready to go on public display. Then they are paraded on the busy streets, where passers-by are persuaded to give their owners a few coins. This is the modern equivalent of the organ-grinder monkeys, but without the annoyance of the tuneless musical accompaniments.

Performing monkeys are still a common sight today, not only in Indonesia, but also in India, Pakistan, Vietnam, China, Japan, Korea and Thailand. On the island of Ko Samui off the east coast of peninsular Thailand, for example, there is a Monkey Theatre where, every day, there is an hour-long performance by large pigtailed macaques, always restrained on collars and leads, that have been diverted from their more serious task of picking coconuts, to entertain paying audiences. The show begins with monkeys sitting on the heads of visitors for the taking of photographs. Then the animals are given placards that they carry around with their names written on them, as a way of introducing themselves. They do this bipedally in a posture that looks highly unnatural for a monkey, but which mimics a human posture and therefore appeals to the onlookers. After this, they do a series of press-ups, as if they are athletes in training. They then perform backward somersaults, followed by a game of basketball during which they show amazing skill at throwing the ball into the net.

At this point, a member of the audience is made to sit on the stage and his hands are tied together. The knot is re-tied about ten times, making it difficult for a human being to release him. A monkey is then brought forward and without hesitation undoes all the knots with remarkable speed and dexterity.

Following this demonstration, a monkey performs a mock weightlifting act, followed by a dramatic fire-juggling act in which a stick that is burning at both ends is twirled round and

All the acts of the performers in the Monkey Theatre mimic human activities, such as weight-lifting.

An unhappy guitar player at the Monkey Theatre.

Selling packets
to the audience.

The finale by the performing macaques of the Monkey Theatre.

round. Two monkeys are then given guitars that they hang around their necks. One of them adopts a vertical, bipedal posture and starts strumming violently, like a rock and roll star. Of all the acts they are encouraged to do, this is the one they like the least, and the strumming monkey at one point flings its guitar down on the ground and refuses to continue. It receives a sharp tap on the top of the head from its keeper, grimaces, and then reluctantly picks up the guitar again, slings the strap over its shoulder and strums noisily once more. When the performance is finally over, it throws the guitar across the stage, letting its trainer know exactly what it thinks of this particular form of entertainment.

Next, a row of tablets is set up across the stage, numbered from one to nine. They are arranged in a random order to make the test more difficult. Then a member of the audience is offered a similar set of tablets, face down so that that numbers are hidden. He selects two and the trainer shows the first of the two to the monkey. It is a number five tablet. The animal then goes along the line on the stage, picks up the number five and takes it to the trainer. This process is then repeated with the number nine, revealing that pigtail macaques are capable of learning and identifying numerals.

The performing monkeys are then given little baskets of packets to sell to members of the audience. If a bank note is placed in one of the animal's baskets, it hands the buyer a packet from the other basket. As a reward, the animals are then each given a sweet liquid in a bowl, but they have to drink it by using a spoon, like a human being consuming a bowl of soup. They do this carefully and with great patience. As a finale, they are given a coconut each and demonstrate their enthusiasm for spinning it, first on the ground and then, while held aloft by a member of the audience. The power and vigour with which they perform this last act illustrates very clearly how they would dislodge a growing nut at the top of a palm tree.

It is undeniably true that this Monkey Theatre reveals to the audience the remarkable tolerance these animals have for being trained to perform unnatural acts, their intelligence and their dexterity, but the general atmosphere is nevertheless one of a demeaning circus performance in which the people watching are primarily enjoying the comic similarity between the monkey actions and human pursuits, rather than the remarkable versatility of these long-suffering primates.

6 Monkeys Exploited

Apart from their roles as pets and performers, monkeys have been exploited in four ways. For many years they have been co-opted as working companions for the collection of food. More recently they have been used as substitutes for astronauts in space exploration and, on a much wider scale, have also been employed as human substitutes in research carried out in medical laboratories. Finally, the latest role they have been made to play is that of service animals – working companions for the disabled.

WORKING COMPANIONS FOR COLLECTING FOOD

For centuries certain monkeys have been exploited as workers in the coconut plantations of the world, helping to gather the heavy nuts from the tall trees. They provide cheap labour on a large scale and must be considered as examples of serious domestic livestock. A prime example of this is to be found today on the island of Ko Samui, off the east coast of peninsular Thailand, an island known as the coconut capital of that country. There are more than 1,000 active coconut plantations on the island and about half of these employ working monkeys. These animals are far more efficient at collecting the nuts from the tops of the palm trees than humans with ropes and ladders.

A working monkey on a coconut plantation on Ko Samui island, Thailand.

Only one species is employed – the pig-tailed macaque, known to the Thais as *lingkang*. The other wild monkey found on the island is the long-tailed macaque and this, it is said, is impossible to train. The pig-tailed species is intelligent and amenable to human handling. Only males are used for nut-picking because they are larger and more powerful than the females. They are allowed to breed in the island's rainforests and the young ones are then trapped, reared and carefully trained.

The training process has three stages. At first, the young male monkey is kept on a collar and lead as a pet, fed and cared for by his owner. During this stage a close bond develops between the animal and his handler. The monkey is well treated and comes to trust his human companion. Then, when he is a little older, he is introduced to coconuts. His owner takes a nut and pierces it through, longways, with an iron rod. While the monkey watches, the man then starts spinning the nut round and round, using the rod as an axis. He does this many times until, one day, the playfulness of the young animal leads to imitation. The monkey tries to copy the owner and, when he succeeds in spinning the nut, is rewarded and praised. Soon he is busily spinning the nut with his hands and feet, faster and faster, until he is completely at ease and familiar with this type of action.

The next phase sees the animal trying to spin a nut that is lying on the ground. Without the iron rod, this is more difficult, but again it is rewarded whenever it shows signs of making these actions. Now comes the second phase of training. The monkey is encouraged to climb to the top of a tall palm tree. Once there, it finds growing coconuts that resist spinning. Puzzled at first, it struggles to turn them and, eventually, manages to twist one far enough to dislodge it. The nut falls to the ground and this event brings more praise and reward. Now the playful nut-spinning of the young monkey gradually becomes transformed into the serious nut-twisting by the adult, and a long period of domestic service has begun.

The third stage is the most difficult. It requires the monkey to learn which nuts are ripe and which are not and to only twist the ripe ones. This is a slow learning process and demands great patience on the part of the trainers. By the time the monkeys are three to four years old, they will have reached their peak of efficiency and are then highly prized. They will continue to work for about another decade and by the time they are retired, each of them will have harvested huge numbers of nuts.

They start each work session by climbing up a tall palm tree on a long lead. They are never allowed off the collar and lead because, if they found themselves completely free, they would probably take off into the rainforest and never be seen again. They may be cooperative workers but they are intelligent enough to know that there is an alternative lifestyle. Once they have finished twisting and dropping the nuts from the first tree, they do not descend to the ground but jump across to a nearby treetop and start work there. Only at the end of a long working session do they come back down to ground level.

In addition to their main task of collecting coconuts, these pigtail macaques are occasionally used to collect other food objects such as mangoes. Today, some of them have also been roped in to support the tourist industry by performing for foreign visitors at one or two of the plantations.

HUMAN SUBSTITUTES IN SPACE

During the early days of the space race, both Russia and the United States employed monkeys as substitutes for astronauts. These early flights were so dangerous that it was considered too risky to send people up in rockets and monkeys were destined to suffer for their genetic closeness to human beings. Inevitably, many of them did not survive.

Between 1948 and 1997 a total of 32 monkeys were rocketed skywards. The United States sent eighteen, Russia twelve and France two. Four species were used, the most popular being the rhesus monkey. In addition there were six squirrel monkeys, two crab-eating macaques and one pig-tailed macaque.

If we accept the official definition of 'space' as being beyond 100 kilometres from earth, then the first monkey in space was a rhesus called Albert II, who reached a height of 134 km (83 miles) on 14 June 1949. Sadly, he did not live to celebrate this momentous event.

Several of the monkeys survived the actual flight but died on their return to earth. The first long-term survivor was a little squirrel monkey called Miss Baker who had travelled at 16,000 km per hour and been subjected to a 32G force in a Jupiter space flight on 28 May 1959. She lived to the ripe old age of 27 and

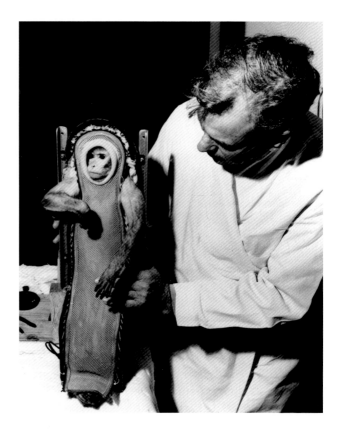

Sam, a rhesus macaque, after his successful ride in the Little Joe 2 spacecraft on 4 December 1959. He reached a height of 53 miles.

did not die until 1984, when she was accorded a formal burial in the grounds of the United States Space & Rocket Center in Huntsville, Alabama.

Sadly, Miss Baker was not typical of these pioneering space monkeys. In general, their chances of survival were poor. Four died due to parachute failure on their return to earth; two died in explosions; one died of suffocation inside its rocket; one died on landing; one was lost at sea after landing; one died of heat

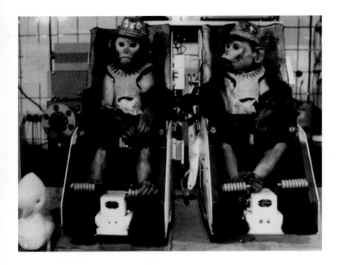

Two rhesus monkeys called Verny and Gordy, who were sent into space in 1985 as part of the Russian-American Biocosmos space programme.

stress while waiting to be recovered; and one died during a biopsy after landing.

Most of the space monkeys were up and back in a single day, but some were sent on much longer missions. Two rhesus monkeys called Zhakonya and Zabiyaka were sent into space by the Russians on 15 September 1989 and did not return until the 28th. They hold the monkey record for a space endurance of thirteen days and seventeen hours.

Another Russian success story concerns a rhesus macaque called Krosh who, after a space journey lasting from 29 December 1992 until 7 January 1993, was later able to mate and produce offspring, a feat that must have been a great relief to future human cosmonauts and astronauts.

If one is disturbed by the thought of the terror that must have been experienced by these 32 monkey space travellers, this has to be balanced against the thought of what would have happened if all these experimental flights had been undertaken instead by human volunteers. The moral dilemma concerning the use of monkeys to stand in for humans in dangerous situations is one that will cause arguments for many years to come. In the case of space exploration, only a very small number of monkeys suffered and saved human lives on an almost one-to-one basis. With that other great exploitation of monkeys – medical research – the situation is very different. Literally millions of monkeys have died in scientific laboratories worldwide, in the service of medical advancement. Many feel this is justified, but others are totally opposed to it. While the debate rages on, here, briefly are the facts.

HUMAN SUBSTITUTES IN LABORATORY EXPERIMENTS

Thousands of monkeys, mostly rhesus macaques and green monkeys, are subjected annually to painful laboratory experiments. The number used each year in the United States is about 60,000; in Europe it is about 10,000. Animal welfare organizations have recently demanded a complete ban on this research, a move that has been met with horror by the medical community.

Those demanding a ban argue that the extreme cruelty involved cannot be justified with such intelligent and sensitive animals. They attack the argument that monkeys must be used because they are so close to humans that results obtained from them can be applied to us. They point out that, if the monkeys are that close, then the procedures performed upon them are tantamount to torture.

In the face of the attacks, scientific research workers have rallied to defend themselves. One scientist has put his point of view succinctly as follows:

I am a surgeon and also a scientist, and part of my work has involved inducing Parkinson's disease in monkeys. My research showed that an area in the brain never previously associated with Parkinson's was overactive, and that operating on it to reduce its activity very significantly reduces the symptoms of Parkinson's. To date around 40,000 people have been helped, following further international research using about 100 monkeys.

In other words, how can you oppose research that has helped 40,000 human sufferers at the cost of only 100 monkeys? If you had a much-loved father, say, with Parkinson's disease, would you deny him medical treatment because it had cost the lives of some experimental monkeys? When the matter becomes personal in this way, most people, even if uneasy about it, would place the health of a loved one above the life of a monkey. Herein lies the dilemma.

Another research scientist makes much the same point:

Primates are the only creatures that suffer from human diseases like Hepatitis C . . . More than 100 million people are now infected with that virus and the effects can be devastating. The key point is that primates provide our only model for developing vaccines. Ban primate research and our hopes of dealing with the scourge of Hepatitis C will vanish.

Others point out that a ban 'would force us to abandon research that could lead to new treatments for Alzheimer's, motor neurone disease, strokes and many other illnesses'.

Opponents of monkey experiments feel that this is all special pleading. They insist that primate research only accounts

Monkeys pictured in an animal research testing laboratory.

for a small percentage of the 96,000 monkeys that are kept in American laboratories:

> Most primates are not used in experiments that study the diseases that kill most Americans. Projects that study primate psychology, alcohol and addictive drugs, brain-mapping, and sex in primates far outnumber studies involving heart disease or cancer.

According to one report, 20,000 monkeys are imported into the United States annually for use in toxicity tests – tests that result in the deaths of the monkeys. Details of these tests are not made available to the public, and animal rights activists have taken to employing undercover agents to obtain these details.

Therefore, a more rigorous restriction on monkey experiments could see the numbers involved dropping dramatically if only essential medical investigations were permitted. However, other opponents of the use of monkeys in laboratory experiments want to go further and remove the monkeys altogether from the equation.

FRAME, the Fund for the Replacement of Animals in Medical Experiments, has issued a report asking for the introduction of alternatives to the use of primates in medical research. They argue that

> Primates are often subjected to invasive and painful procedures and are restricted to a lifetime of laboratory incarceration: thus it is increasingly unethical to pursue such inadequate 'models' of human illness.

Their report makes the point that

Tetra, a rhesus macaque, the first successfully cloned monkey using the technique of embryo-splitting. Tetra was born at the Oregon National Primate Research Centre in 1999.

It was claimed there were no alternatives to animal tests on cosmetics, but when these tests were banned, the industry quickly found alternatives. Banning primate experiments would concentrate scientists' minds in exactly the same way.

Protesters also argue that

Other approaches are now more likely to lead to the development of new drugs and treatments: cultures of human cells grown in laboratories, for example. These technologies could now take over the use of primates in research.

And so the debate goes on.

Legislation may soon be introduced that will settle the matter, at least in Europe. Members of the European Parliament, following an outright ban on the use of great apes, such as chimpanzees, in medical research, are now considering the banning of the use of all monkey species as well. This will stop what critics have described as the prolonged abuse of monkeys, but some aspects of vital medical research will, inevitably, be curtailed as a result.

In America, the more extreme opponents of monkey experiments, fearing that no such legislation will be forthcoming there, have recently taken the battle to a new level. In Los Angeles, they have demonstrated outside the homes of research scientists working with monkeys; they have put a Molotov cocktail on the porch of one house, caused a flood in another, placed a bomb under the car of another and firebombed yet another.[1] Violent protests have also flared up elsewhere and, in some instances, special protection has had to be provided for research workers.

This is clearly not a matter that will be resolved quickly. Scientists would do well to limit their use of monkeys to studies that have special merit for human health. And their opponents would do well to remember that the research workers they are firebombing are also primates that deserve protection.

WORKING COMPANIONS FOR THE DISABLED

Recent years have seen the development of a new form of monkey exploitation in which the animals are trained to be the slaves of humans with extreme forms of physical disability.[2] The monkeys used are the intelligent capuchins from Central and South

America. They are taken as infants from a special captive breeding colony and hand-reared in a human home, so that they are accustomed to human company and to that particular kind of environment. This rearing process is lengthy, usually lasting from three to five years. They are then put through a long, rigorous training regime in which they develop the kinds of skills that will be of help to humans suffering from extreme forms of immobility.

Unfortunately for the trainers, capuchins vary a great deal in their individual personalities. Some are too boisterous, some too unreliable, some slightly aggressive, and so on. Only a fraction of those that have been carefully hand-reared will turn out to have the quiet, friendly, steady temperament required for this specialized type of work. The others have to be rejected from the scheme.

When the ultra-cooperative ones have been fully trained, they are then placed with severely disabled individuals who are incapable of carrying out even the simplest household tasks themselves. A series of simple commands to the monkeys will trigger appropriate responses, and the level of intelligence and manual skill displayed by some of these trained capuchins is truly remarkable.

Among the actions performed by the best of these expert monkey 'helpers' are the cooking of food in a microwave, opening bottles, getting food out of the refrigerator, flicking light switches on or off, pushing control buttons, turning the pages of a book, picking up dropped objects, operating a DVD player, and even washing the faces of their helpless human companions or feeding them with a spoon.

The non-profit American organization supplying these service monkeys is called 'Helping Hands'. It began operating in 1979 and has since gone from strength to strength, placing more and more monkey helpers each year. The success of its operation is reflected in the fact that some of the monkey-human

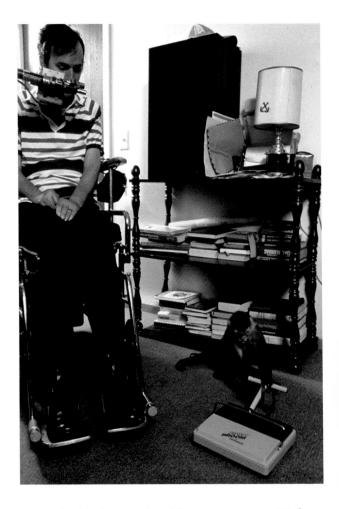

A number of capuchin monkeys have successfully been trained to act as helpers for the severely disabled.

companionships have now lasted for over twenty years. It is fortunate that the capuchin monkey has an unusually long lifespan.

The first service monkey was a capuchin called Hellion, paired up with a quadriplegic named Robert Foster who had lost the use of his limbs in a car crash. Foster was able to point out what he wanted Hellion to do using a mouth-operated laser. The monkey's tasks included combing his hair, placing food in his mouth, locking doors, working the stereo and even cleaning the floor with a scaled-down vacuum. Amazingly, their close partnership lasted for 28 years, until Robert Foster died in 2007. Hellion outlived him by four years, dying in July 2011.

Inevitably, there have been animal welfare voices raised against this practice. Critics have warned that, as they grow older, even the most docile capuchins may become unpredictable, aggressive and messy. Despite this, the Helping Hands organization claims an 80 per cent success rate in pairing individual animals with their owners. Other critics say that the whole idea of operating 'service monkeys' is unfair to the capuchins, to which one of the paralysed men who was enjoying the independence provided by his companion monkey tellingly replied: 'I wonder how many of these critics are severely disabled.'

7 Monkey Quotations

As central themes in literary works, monkeys are almost non-existent. If a primate is going to appear as a leading character in a book or a film, he will always be a great ape – usually a chimpanzee, but sometimes a gorilla or an orang-utan. In literary circles the monkey has always been overshadowed by these impressive apes, and has been viewed by authors as useful only as a minor amusement where an exotic pet is needed, or a little domestic chaos is called for. It is much the same in the realm of proverbs and quotations. Some animals have inspired rich collections of quotable phrases and sayings, but not the monkey.

One of the few monkey quotes that does exist may go some way to explaining this. In 1820 the English wit Henry Luttrell commented: 'I dislike monkeys – they always remind me of poor relations.' In other words, if we are going to start thinking about them and their attributes, they are likely to embarrass us.

A little later, in 1862, the American clergyman Henry Ward Beecher proclaimed that 'the monkey is an organized sarcasm on the human race'. This remark was made three years after Darwin had published *The Origin of Species*, and Beecher, rather surprisingly, was a supporter of Darwin's work. It is as if he is saying that, in its newfound evolutionary importance, the monkey can be seen as cutting mankind down to size.

Gabriel von Max,
Monkey Reading,
1915, oil on panel.

A bespectacled monkey in the window of a New Orleans antiques shop.

Perhaps the most famous quote involving monkeys is the one that states: 'give a monkey a typewriter and if it keeps hitting the keys randomly for long enough it will eventually type out the works of Shakespeare'. This idea has amused mathematicians who say that, although not impossible in theory, this feat would take longer than 100,000 times the age of the universe. So, for anyone wishing to sit watching this typing monkey at work, patience would be a virtue.

As an example of 'performance art', lecturers at Plymouth University did indeed provide a group of six captive macaques with a computer keyboard to see what would happen. After a month, the zoo monkeys had produced five pages of typing, mostly of the letter *s*.

In recent times the idea of monkeys typing Shakespeare has become the source of a whole host of jokes. One speaker exclaimed: 'We've heard that a million monkeys at a million keyboards could produce the complete works of Shakespeare; now, thanks to the Internet, we know that is not true.' Another said, 'I heard someone tried the monkeys-on-typewriters experiment, trying for the plays of Shakespeare, but all they got were the collected works of Francis Bacon.' And another: 'I heard that if you locked William Shakespeare in a room with a typewriter for long enough he'd eventually write all the songs by the Monkees.'

Other monkey quotes fall into two categories: those that see the innocently simple monkey as somehow superior to the deviously complex human; and those that see the monkey as an essentially inferior being.

In the first category are the following: 'Monkeys are superior to men in this: when a monkey looks into a mirror he sees a monkey.' And: 'Monkeys who very sensibly refrain from speech lest they should be set to earn their livings.' A later variant of this was 'He knows when not to talk, which is the biggest asset the monkey possesses over the human.' And a West African proverb that states: 'No monkey ever laughs at another'.

The words of the song 'Three monkeys sitting under a coconut tree' include the following refrain:

There's a strange rumour that can't be true.
They say man was descended from our noble race,
But the very idea is a big disgrace.
No monkey ever deserted his wife
Or her baby to ruin their lives.

Quotes seeing the monkey as representing an inferior state include Emerson's comment that 'slavery is an institution for converting men into monkeys'. Mark Twain said: 'I believe the heavenly Father invented man because he was disappointed in the monkey.' And several politicians, including Winston Churchill, have been credited with stating: 'Never hold discussions with the monkey when the organ-grinder is in the room.'

And finally, the great English physicist Stephen Hawking puts both monkey and man firmly in their place when he wrote: 'We are just an advanced breed of monkey on a minor planet of a very average star.'

If we are an advanced monkey, then it follows that the monkey is a backward version of us. This view, translated into body language, has been in the news in 2012 when a football supporter was being sought by the police because they wanted to prosecute him for making a 'monkey gesture' during a match, hooting and curling his arms in the direction of a black player of the opposing team. This was officially described as a 'racist gesture', which of course it is not. It is a 'species gesture' and would only be insulting if one were convinced that humans are superior to monkeys.

The truth is that, in the tropical treetops, monkeys are far superior to men, even if, in cities, they are not. In other words, instead of considering monkeys either superior or inferior to men, we should see them simply as different from one another.

8 Monkeys and Artists

The monkey has never been a major preoccupation of artists. Where animals are concerned, it is the domesticated breeds that have always been strongly favoured. For every monkey portrait, there are a thousand paintings of dogs or horses. With wildlife artists, the same is true of lions and elephants. Despite this, there have been some remarkable exceptions,[1] from Pisanello in the fifteenth century to Picasso in the twentieth. As there is no overall theme – some artists representing the monkey as a symbol, others depicting it simply as itself – the best approach here is to discuss monkey paintings artist by artist, in historical order, and examine each one on its own terms.

PISANELLO (1395–1455)

One of the first major artists to focus his attention on the monkey as a subject was Antonio Pisanello, an Italian who was working at the very beginning of the Renaissance. He has been described as 'the first universal Humanist among artists' and his skilfully accurate sketches of monkeys in naturalistic poses could easily be the work of a modern wildlife artist of the twentieth century. There is no hint here of the religious symbolism that had dominated monkey portrayals in previous centuries. These are not the monkeys of parables or fables, or of religious allegories. These are monkeys as monkeys, with no moral messages attached.

Pisanello's drawings, made mostly in the late 1440s, have been carefully preserved in the *Codex Vallardi*, now housed in the Louvre in Paris. The monkeys are shown in a variety of postures, standing alert, hugging themselves, squatting miserably or sleeping. Pisanello was one of the first artists ever to sit and draw directly from nature, and it shows. His advanced draughtsmanship makes the illustrations of monkeys that appeared in the great natural history volumes of the centuries that followed look stilted and old fashioned.

Pisanello's drawings of the late 1440s show monkeys in a variety of postures.

In the early part of the fifteenth century, it was fashionable for princely houses to maintain a menagerie of exotic birds and mammals, and Pisanello undoubtedly made his sketches in one of those. This is evident from the waist-belts worn by some of the monkeys, indicating that they were captive specimens.

A famous engraving made in 1498 by the German master Dürer, known as *The Virgin with the Monkey,* has intrigued experts for years. The Madonna and the infant Jesus on her lap are depicted in a traditional way, but the addition of a tethered monkey by her right foot is unorthodox, to say the least. The Virgin sits on a low wooden fence and it is to this that the monkey is attached by a cord that goes around its waist.

The idea that this monkey is meant to be a pet belonging to Mary seems ridiculous. All art historians who have commented on this strange scene are in agreement that this animal is not present as itself but as a symbol of something else. The engraving was done at a period when animals were often introduced into a composition to act as symbolic messages about the rest of the scene and there can be little doubt that this is the case here too.

One historian sees the monkey as symbolizing the basest animal instincts of man and believes that it is shown tethered to confirm that the Virgin Mary's great power for good has reduced it to a subdued captive. Another comments that 'the shackled monkey represents the prison of secular pleasures'. Yet another regards the monkey as a symbol of lewdness, greed and gluttony, all of which are defeated by the Virgin's holiness because the tethered monkey is helpless. Finally, another interprets the role of the monkey as a symbolic representation of the way that the Virgin's purity has conquered and subdued the Devil.

These interpretations differ very little from one another and make good sense, but Dürer has failed to portray the monkey as having any of these base attributes. It looks too skinny to be greedy, too sick to be lecherous, and too docile to be devilish. It seems as if Dürer, when he was creating the work, rather liked the monkey and enjoyed drawing it. He has given it facial markings

Albrecht Dürer's engraving *The Virgin with the Monkey*, 1498, has intrigued experts for years: the Madonna and Child are depicted traditionally, but the addition of a monkey is a surprise.

that, although slightly exaggerated, are clearly based on the vervet monkey, one of the commonest of all African species and one that he may well have seen in northern Europe, even at this early date, kept by someone as an exotic pet. Its mood is one of quiet restraint and gives no hint of the evil qualities for which it is supposed to stand. One can only suppose that the Virgin's gentle power has removed all its animalistic qualities and left it as a compliant, if rather sad friend.

The idea that Dürer liked the monkey more than perhaps he should have done is borne out by the fact that some years later, in 1520, when he was on a visit to the Netherlands, he saw a young Barbary macaque and was prepared to pay as much as five golden guilders for it, a sum that today would be more than £350. Many of his drawings and paintings reveal that, as an artist, he could not suppress his love for his animal subjects and his respect for them in their own right rather than as mere symbols.

PIETER BRUEGEL (1525–1569)

The Flemish master Pieter Bruegel the Elder created an unusual painting in which two monkeys were the only figures. This was unusual because most earlier portrayals of monkeys relegated them to small details in larger compositions. In Bruegel's rather sad scene, painted in 1562, the two animals are seen squatting forlornly on a broad stone windowsill, with heavy chains secured around their waists. These chains are both attached to a central ring, making it impossible for the monkeys ever to avoid one another. The location has been identified as a gable window in Antwerp's Fort Philippe, and there is a panorama of the city visible in the distance. As if to emphasize the wretched incarceration of the monkeys, two birds are visible, soaring through the sky beyond the fort.

Art historians have claimed that Bruegel is offering us a double message with this sombre work. The first is that we humans are superior to nature, as represented by the two monkeys. We can capture it, enslave it and exploit it as we wish. This was the teaching of the Church at the time, embodied in the phrase 'brute beasts of no understanding' when referring to animal life. It is suggested that Bruegel was bewailing this entrenched religious attitude towards nature.

Pieter Bruegel, *Two Monkeys*, 1562, wood on panel.

Alternatively, it is argued that Bruegel, like many other artists, may have been employing the monkeys as symbolic of the human

condition. There they sit, held firm by their chains, like wretched humans trapped by the chains of injustice and the cruelties of society. More specifically, they could have been meant to symbolize the domination of the Netherlands by the Spanish.

A simpler explanation is that there is no subtext, but that the artist, on observing two pet monkeys in his home city of Antwerp, was intrigued by their shape and their markings and simply sat down to paint the portraits of two unusual captive sitters. He has paid great attention to their appearance, so that it is possible to identify them as collared mangabeys (*Cercocebus torquatus*) from West Africa. In the year that he painted this particular picture, Antwerp was engaged in an important sugar trade with that part of Africa and sailors' pet monkeys would have been available to purchase from time to time as an exotic oddity: one clearly that caught Bruegel's imagination.

GEORGE STUBBS (1724–1806)

Although most famous for his brilliant studies of horses, George Stubbs also included other animals in his repertoire. His remarkable portrayal of a monkey, painted in 1774, shows the animal caught in the act of picking a peach. The pile of peaches at the bottom right-hand corner of the picture suggests that the monkey is in the process of building up a supply of these exotic fruits.

Stubbs gave the painting the vague title of *Portrait of a Monkey*. A quarter of a century later, for some unknown reason, he made a precise copy of this work and this time called it simply *A Monkey*.[2] Both of these versions were shown by him at the Royal Academy in London. The earlier 1774 painting is slightly superior to the later 1798 one, expert opinion commenting that 'there is a far more powerful sense of immediate observation from life in the earlier version'.[3]

Many years later, the title *The Green Monkey* was introduced by someone whose scientific knowledge of monkey species was clearly lacking because, apart from other differences, green monkeys have black faces. In fact, the animal portrayed is a young macaque, probably a crab-eating macaque from South-East Asia, and peaches are not part of its natural diet. Despite the exotic setting, the picture was almost certainly based on a captive monkey in a patron's private menagerie or on an exotic pet being kept as a novelty by a citizen of eighteenth-century London. As with all Stubbs's animal portraits, there is an almost painful sense of anatomical accuracy about this work and, despite the artistic presence of the luscious peaches, the monkey's body looks disturbingly undernourished.

MORI SOSEN (1747–1821)

In the late eighteenth and early nineteenth century there was an exceptional Japanese artist whose paintings of monkeys showed a deep understanding of their anatomy, movements, postures and behaviour that went far beyond anything his rivals could produce. Mori Sosen was a master at conveying the character and lifestyle of the Japanese macaque. He spent a great deal of time studying the actions of these monkeys in their natural forest habitat, and became so addicted to them that he rarely depicted anything else in his technically exquisite paintings. He would occasionally portray deer or wild boar, but the macaques were his lasting obsession.

Sosen's special achievement was to create the precise texture of the monkey's fur using deft, delicate brush strokes, and the movements of his animals were always lively and 'of the moment'. Sadly, because his work became so popular, many second-rate imitations have appeared, displaying inferior skills and perhaps, as a result, damaging his reputation in the West.

George Stubbs, *Portrait of a Monkey*, 1774, oil on panel.

Mori Sosen,
Japanese Macaque,
1800, painting on
silk scroll.

The French primitive artist Henri Rousseau is also widely known as *Le Douanier*, which is usually translated as 'the customs officer'. This is slightly misleading because, in reality, his day job was that of a Parisian tax collector. He was not at the border, checking people trying to enter the country, but instead was busy demanding toll payments for foodstuffs and tobacco entering the capital from the countryside. He was also a petty criminal and an audacious egotist, but none of that matters when you set eyes on his magical paintings.

His passion was his art, and he devoted his spare time to creating some of the greatest 'outsider' landscapes ever seen. In his day, his self-taught paintings were ridiculed, but he is now recognized as probably the greatest naive artist in recent history. In particular, he was obsessed with exotic jungle scenes in which

Henri Rousseau,
Exotic Landscape,
1910, oil on canvas.

the dense foliage was punctuated with wild animals of many kinds. These jungles were entirely imaginary. Throughout his entire life he never left France and the nearest he came to wild animals was at the old Paris zoo at the Jardin des Plantes.

In 1910, he completed several massive compositions in which his jungles are populated with monkeys. In one of these paintings, four of these animals are shown raiding an orange tree. Two are hanging in mid-air. One has fallen to the ground, still clutching its orange, and we can see only its sprawling arms and legs. A fourth sits on the ground, already starting to devour its succulent prize. There are two species depicted here – pink-faced ones on the left and a black-faced one on the right.

Of the black-faced monkey, Rousseau wrote in his personal album that:

> Aside from what we have said about the Hindu worship of this animal, we must add that the langurs or leaf monkeys are so accustomed to following their whims that they truly seem to command it like masters.

The atmosphere of the scene depicted in this work is that of an innocent paradise, a joyful Garden of Eden without any troublesome human intervention. A friend of the artist is quoted as saying that Rousseau was 'brimming with love for creatures and things, and there was so much peace, so much sunlight that no sadness could grab hold of him'.[4]

PAUL GAUGUIN (1848–1903)

In 1893 the French Post-Impressionist artist Paul Gauguin painted a portrait of his model, known as Annah the Javanese, with a pet monkey sitting at her feet. At first sight, one could be forgiven for thinking that this is another of the famously exotic scenes created by the artist after he abandoned Europe for the island of Tahiti in the South Pacific. This is not, however, the case and the painting has a very different origin.

Gauguin left for Tahiti in 1891 and spent two years there. In 1893 he returned to Paris and set up a studio where he painted for two years before finally returning to the South Pacific in 1895. It was during this short interlude in Paris that he acquired the Javanese model he called Annah. He bought the monkey as a present for the girl. Both lived with him in his studio and it was there that he created this portrait.

Annah had been sent to Paris from Southeast Asia as a gift for a French opera singer. The girl was found by the police wandering about the Gare de Lyon with the singer's address written on a label that was tied around her neck, as if she were an undelivered parcel. Taken to the singer to work for her as a servant, she was soon dismissed and ended up as a model posing naked for Gauguin. Although only thirteen, she soon became his mistress.

In his studio Gauguin seems to have given considerable freedom to the lively if unhappy monkey. An artist visiting the studio wrote:

> In the middle of the room, a perpetually moving monkey was climbing up and down a rope that hung from the ceiling. Underneath, on the floor, sat a small woman with a yellowish-dark complexion, wearing a blue cotton frock. Silently smiling; it was the artist's mistress.[5]

In winter the studio was too cold for the monkey, which suffered as a result. 'A shivering monkey was curled up among the easels and, in this exotic environment . . . one felt very far from Paris', wrote another visitor to his studio.[6]

Annah caused a scandal when she danced naked with her monkey at parties given by Gauguin, but the artist delighted in

showing them both off to his guests. He also took the girl and her monkey with him on a trip to Brittany. There, she was attacked by the locals as a witch. They threw stones at her and Gauguin became involved in a fracas during which his leg was broken. On the way to the local hospital, Annah wept hysterically and the monkey shrieked in excitement. Gauguin and the girl quarrelled and she and the monkey left for Paris, where she ransacked his studio and left.

The monkey depicted by Gauguin has brick-red fur and a pale blue face-mask, with a hint of white at the throat. With this combination of colours, Gauguin has set us a puzzle, because he has given the animal the red coat of a patas monkey, but combined it with the blue face of a guenon. The blue face seems to be the more reliable feature, although there is clearly some artistic licence at work here.

FRANCIS PICABIA (1879–1953)

Francis Picabia was a leading figure in the chaotically rebellious Dada art movement during the early part of the twentieth century. He was one of the avant-garde artists who were disgusted with the European establishment for allowing the horrific slaughter of the First World War. Their disgust took the form of an attempt to undermine all forms of traditional art, custom and morality.

In 1920, Picabia produced a savage attack on three respected artists, an irreverent assault that portrayed each of the great men as a monkey with its tail between its legs. The work, entitled *Portrait of Cezanne, Portrait of Renoir, Portrait of Rembrandt; Still Life*, consisted of a stuffed monkey attached to a canvas, with its title written in capital letters all around it.

Portraying these recognized masters as monkeys was clearly intended to be a major insult, and places Picabia's monkey firmly

Paul Gauguin, *Annah the Javanese*, 1893, oil on canvas.

Francis Picabia, *Still Lifes: Portrait of Cézanne, Portrait of Renoir, Portrait of Rembrandt*, 1920, mixed media on cardboard.

in the symbolic role of the animal seen as a foolish caricature of human existence. Although a genuine attack on traditional art, the work was also meant to be seen as a joke. In fact, the following year, Picabia abandoned the Dada movement because it was starting to take itself too seriously. In his farewell address he said: 'Dada, you see, was not serious . . . and if certain people take it seriously now, it's because it is dead! . . . One must be a nomad, pass through ideas like one passes through countries and cities.'

Pablo Picasso loved the circus and, in 1901, when he was only twenty years old, he had visited a monkey circus, the *Cirque Medrano*, that had come to Paris, after which he produced a work called *Clown and Monkey*. A few years later, in 1905, he returned to this theme, creating a large sketch that would become one of his most famous early works. A tender scene, it shows us a remarkably tame and friendly male baboon gazing compassion-ately at a family of young circus performers. The implication is that, not only did the animal and the acrobats work side by side in the circus, but they had also become an extended family group. Far from being jealous of the new infant, the monkey gives the impression that it would defend the baby and its par-ents against outsiders. This baboon, Picasso seems to be saying, is not a dangerous pet, but a loyal bodyguard.

Because, in reality, an adult male baboon can easily become violent, no matter how well trained it is, Picasso's gentle treat-ment of the animal was at odds with the words of the great French naturalist the Comte de Buffon, who had written in the eighteenth century that a monkey 'is lively, its temperament hot, its nature petulant, so none of its feelings are mitigated by edu-cation. All its habits are excessive and more closely resemble the actions of a lunatic than of a man.' Although Picasso would not have agreed with these words, this did not stop him providing the illustrations for a later edition of Buffon, in 1936, when once again he portrayed a friendly baboon, this time in the act of offer-ing a morsel of food and with a faint smile on its face.

Picasso portrayed monkeys on a number of occasions through-out his long career and clearly felt a kinship with them. As a young man he is thought to have kept several as pets. As an old man, when he was asked by a journalist to comment on a report that a chimpanzee had been painting pictures that had then been exhibited in a London gallery, Picasso left the room briefly, then returned, swinging his arms like a monkey, leapt at the reporter and bit him. He could hardly have made his feelings of affinity with simians more clear.

In 1951 Picasso created a bronze sculpture called *Baboon and Young*. What makes this work so remarkable are the unpromising materials he employed when constructing it, before it was cast in bronze. They were no more than common objects lying around his studio in which the artist saw visual possibilities that others would have missed.

Picasso's art dealer had bought his young son, Claude, two small toy cars, a Panhard and a Renault. Although the four-year-old Claude was most unhappy to see his toys being taken away, Picasso commandeered them and placed the Renault upside-down underneath the Panhard to form the head of the baboon. The front of the upper car became the long snout of the animal and its roof became the top of the skull. Two eyes were placed inside the windscreen. The gap between the upper and the lower car became the slightly opened mouth of the monkey. The front of the lower car became the lower jaw. Two pitcher handles found in a nearby scrapheap were used to make the ears. A large, round jug was added to make the baboon's body, with the two jug handles forming the animal's shoulders. To make the long tail, he used an old car-spring with a rolled end. The other details of the figure were then modelled to complete the sculpture.

When this odd assortment of everyday materials was then cast in bronze, the result was a powerful image of a standing baboon protectively clasping its tiny offspring to its chest. Picasso had successfully transformed a group of humble objects into a powerful sculptural image – an image he referred to as 'the ancestor'. What his little son Claude would have thought, had he known

Pablo Picasso, *The Acrobat's Family with a Monkey*, 1905, mixed media on cardboard.

that his toy cars would fetch nearly $7 million when sold at auction in 2002, is hard to imagine.

A few years later, in 1954, Picasso produced a series of 180 sketches that once again featured monkeys.[7] In one of them, an attractive young girl reclines against a wall with her legs apart. Lying in her lap is her tame monkey, dressed in a long frilly ruff and a short frilly skirt. The monkey, clasping the girl's knee and her neck, is twisting its head round to look at an apple she is holding. The smiling girl's eyes glance down at her pet to see if it will make a grab for the apple. If the monkey were a male, this would be a grotesque parody of Eve offering the apple to Adam in the Garden of Eden, but the swollen rear-end of the animal reveals that it is, in fact, a female in heat.

This, the last and best sketch in his long series, like many of the others, reminds us of Picasso's visual love affair with the circus and circus folk. Both the girl and her monkey, by their attire, are circus performers who are presumably resting between shows. There is a relaxed, friendly intimacy between the girl and her animal that is almost erotic, emphasized by the way the monkey is positioned between her legs, but this sexual element is not allowed to overpower the predominantly innocent atmosphere of the scene.

MAX ERNST (1891–1976)

The German Surrealist Max Ernst rarely included monkeys in his works, but in one remarkable painting of 1922, *Blue Monkey with Flower*, he featured a detailed portrait of one as the centrepiece of his composition. This strange painting, almost but not quite a straightforward simian portrait, has given rise to much debate concerning its true meaning.

One school of thought sees the blue monkey as a self-portrait of the artist as an alchemist.[8] As a self-portrait, it certainly has Ernst's piercing blue eyes, a feature of the man commented upon by his friends. Significantly, if you compare the portrait with a photograph of a blue monkey, it is clear that the artist deliberately altered the true colour of the monkey's eyes to match his own. Ernst shows the natural colouring of a blue monkey with reasonable accuracy except for the eyes and the cheeks. In the living monkey the cheeks are blue-grey and the eyes pale orange. In the portrait these colours are deliberately switched, the cheeks becoming orange and the eyes blue. So the argument for this being a quirky self-portrait seems sound enough.

The connection to alchemy is more tenuous, although in the bottom left corner one can just see a burning furnace where, presumably, an alchemist was busily turning the lead of nature into the gold of art – just as Ernst had turned the natural monkey into a strange self-portrait. In fact, Ernst himself once talked about 'the alchemy of collage', in which the artist turns the dross of advertisements and other readymade images into exciting new visual statements. Also, if he were aware of Grandville's monkey scenes in which the animal becomes a symbol of imitation, it would make sense, because alchemists sought to create imitations of the works of nature, as do many artists.

Ernst dedicated the monkey painting to Cécile, the four-year-old daughter of the woman with whom he had just started an affair – the woman who would later become Salvador Dalí's wife – Gala. In a photograph taken in the summer of 1922, there is a record of them together that shows Cécile hugging a soft toy that appears to be a large monkey – no doubt the inspiration for the painting.[9]

The British artist Graham Sutherland produced several works entitled *Monkey*, but they usually depicted one of the great apes – the orang-utan. Between 1965 and 1968, however, he set about creating his own bestiary, in which he did include a true monkey. The idea had come to him when he was visiting the Cloisters Museum in New York, where he saw a medieval bestiary.

> He had also studied a catalogue of these compendia of real and fabulous beasts, called *Constant Companions,* from an exhibition in 1964 in Houston, Texas. Such a subject, he thought, might lend itself to his preoccupation with the affinities between men, animals and machines.[10]

There were 26 prints in Sutherland's bestiary and the one he called *Pink Monkey*, completed in 1968, shows us a dignified baboon with a pink and gold cape of hair, sitting, not in a natural environment, but rather forlornly on a wooden crate in a bleak cell. This is an adult baboon, but without the usual sexual details, gazing blankly into the distance, apparently resigned to a life of stultifying boredom in captivity.

FRIDA KAHLO (1907–1954)

Born in Mexico, Frida Kahlo was involved in a road accident when she was a teenager. The bus she was travelling on was struck by a tram and she became impaled on a shaft of metal that went through her, she said, 'like a sword into a bull'. Her spine was broken in three places, her pelvis was fractured, and she nearly died. The accident robbed her of any chance of having children and condemned her to a life of pain. During

Max Ernst
*Blue Monkey
with Flower,* 1922,
oil on canvas.

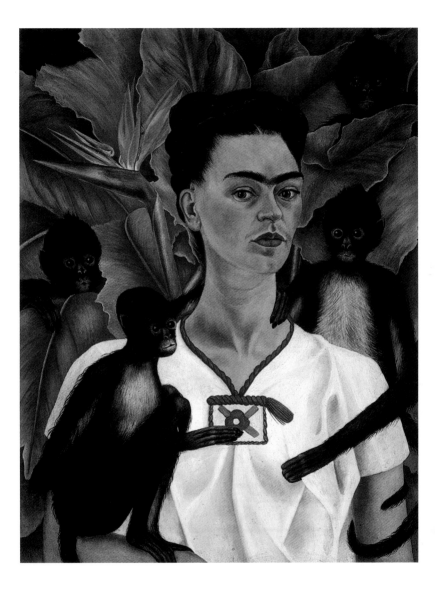

her slow recovery she started to paint and poured her feelings about her predicament into her work, giving her imagery a poignant intensity.

Between 1938 and 1945 Kahlo painted several portraits of herself with monkeys. In the most successful of these she is seen surrounded by four spider monkeys in a lush tropical setting. One sits on her right arm and clings to her neck, like a friendly pet, while another wraps its prehensile tail around her left arm and holds tightly to her clothing. Two more peep out of the foliage behind her. Her posture is stiff and her expression one of resigned stoicism. There is no hint of tenderness towards the animals or of maternal affection for them. It is almost as if she is pretending that they are not there.

This strange painting has given rise to much speculation. It is known that her husband, the Mexican artist Diego Rivera, gave her a pet spider monkey as a substitute for the child she desperately wanted but could not have. It was named Fulang Chang and she also had another called Caimito de Guayabal. In real life she is said to have treasured these pets and doted on them, but in the painting the way she portrays her relationship with them does not reflect this. In the picture it is they who are gently protecting her, not she who is caring for them.

It is as if the painting is hinting that these surrogate children, although much loved, are failing to satisfy her maternal feelings, and are perhaps unavoidably accentuating the absence of the real thing. Viewed in this way, her erect posture and apparent lack of interest in the monkeys emphasizes her steely determination to soldier on despite her childless state. She presents us with a contradiction, showing herself as literally wrapped around by natural forces, in an intimate association with flora and fauna, and yet standing aloof from them because of her unnatural, barren condition.

Frida Kahlo, *Self-portrait with Monkeys*, 1943, oil on canvas.

In the end, the only offspring Kahlo had to offer us were her attractive but sinister paintings. André Breton summed it up when he said of her work: 'The art of Frida Kahlo is a ribbon around a bomb.'

FRANCIS BACON (1909–1992)

Francis Bacon is best known for his tortured studies of the human figure, but from time to time he turned his attention to other species, including one memorable image of a baboon. Called simply *Study of a Baboon*, it was painted in 1953. It shows the animal squatting on the fork of a dead tree, with the wire of a zoo enclosure behind it. The head is tilted back and the jaws are wide open so that the baboon appears to be screaming at the heavens, as if tormented by its captivity. It is like a simian version of Bacon's famously screaming popes of 1951.

Some years after he painted this picture, and knowing me as a zoologist, he asked whether I thought he had caught the animal's pose correctly. I assured him that he had done so and he replied: 'Yes, I think I have got the scream, but I am having terrible trouble with the smile.' An exhaustive survey of his paintings confirms that, although there are many screaming figures, there is, indeed, not a single smile to be seen anywhere.

Without knowing its precise source, one could hazard a guess that Bacon would have copied his baboon from a photograph, found in a newspaper, magazine or book, or perhaps taken by himself. Photographs had always been a major source of images for him. When his mother had moved to South Africa, he visited her three times, in 1950, 1952 and 1957, and while there he spent many hours in the Kruger National Park, watching and photographing the wildlife. He wrote that 'I felt and memorized the excitement of seeing animals move through long grass.'[11] It has

Francis Bacon,
Study of a Baboon,
1953, oil on canvas.

been suggested that, back in London in 1953, one of his own snapshots of a Kruger Park baboon was the inspiration for this painting. Although his observations of baboons in Africa may have focused his interest on this type of animal, it is more likely that the true source of this particular image was a photograph he found in one of his favourite books, Marius Maxwell's *Stalking Big Game with a Camera in Equatorial Africa*, published in 1925. In the plate that shows baboons in acacia trees, the animal on the right is sitting in a forked tree very much like the one shown in Bacon's painting.

Significantly, he has felt the need to add details of a cage to his composition – a device he also used frequently with his human figures, even his popes. And we, the viewers of the work, find ourselves inside the cage with this ferocious-looking animal, making its close proximity a matter for some concern.

The problem with taking images from photographs is that photographs are silent. If an animal, like this baboon, has its mouth wide open it is impossible to guess what noise is accompanying the action. Bacon told me that his baboon was screaming, but I was not so sure. Out of politeness, however, I refrained from pointing out to him that, in reality, it was more likely to be yawning. This is because, when screaming, a baboon aims its head straight at the cause of its anger, but when yawning it may tilt its head backwards, as is the case here. To the uninitiated, a photograph of a yawning baboon may well appear to be showing an angry monkey in the act of screeching or roaring its distress. Without the accompanying sound effects this distinction might not be clear.

Despite this, however, Bacon's painting remains a hauntingly powerful image. Whether the animal is yawning with the intense boredom of captivity, or howling to the skies its protest at being held a prisoner, is a matter for the viewers of this remarkable painting to decide for themselves. And, either way, there is no escaping the fact that, as they look at the painting, they find themselves worryingly near to an animal that owns a massive pair of jaws and huge fangs.

9 Monkeys as Animals

Each group of animals has a few special features that are the secret of its success. In the case of monkeys there are three: their hands, their eyes and their brains. Their hands have evolved opposable thumbs, enabling them to grasp small branches when leaping through the trees, and sensitive, flattened nails that improve precision when holding small objects. Their eyes have moved round to the front of the head, giving them the binocular vision that is so valuable when judging distances. As vision has come to dominate their world, so the sense of smell has been reduced, resulting in a greatly flattened face. This has also given them the chance of evolving a whole range of facial expressions indicating their changing moods.[1] Finally, their brains have become more advanced, providing them with a greater level of intelligence that allows them to solve their survival problems without resorting to muscle-power. To sum up, their evolutionary motto might be: sleight of hand, 3D vision and brain before brawn.

Armed with these advantages, monkeys have spread right across the warmer regions of the world. In the past, when these regions were more thickly forested, monkeys will have been even more successful than they are today. But the ever-increasing human demand for wood, fed by the global logging industry, and the massive spread of agriculture, have greatly reduced their natural habitats and their numbers are in decline in many areas.

Monkeys have evolved a whole range of facial expressions, demonstrated here by a threatening rhesus monkey, a stump-tailed macaque sticking its tongue out in a greeting called 'lip-smacking', and a gelada baboon (below) which, despite its appearance, is nervously friendly.

Scampering high into the trees at the first sign of danger.

A taste for bushmeat in some tropical countries has also had a damaging impact, as has the Western demand for laboratory specimens for medical research.

However, despite all these growing challenges, most species of monkeys have managed to survive reasonably well, largely because of their primary defence mechanism, namely scampering high into the trees at the first threat of danger. They are so nimble that few predators have any hope of catching them. Their main enemies are some of the larger eagles, snakes and cats. If they come down from the trees and try to cross rivers, then crocodiles may become a problem. Apart from that, there are really only human hunters to worry about, and in parts of Africa an occasional raiding party of chimpanzees.

The monkeys themselves, with their alert eyes and ears and their slender, athletic bodies, are always ready to flee at the first sign of danger. Aiding them in this is a variety of alarm calls. They always move about in small groups. If one member of a group senses danger, it will immediately sound the alarm, and they all then rush to safety. In some species there are several different kinds of alarm calls, each sound giving information about which type of danger is present. Some alarm calls are soft coughs or barks intended to alert the other monkeys but without advertising the position of the group far and wide. Others are loud screams or hoots that throw caution to the wind.[2]

Although typical monkeys live in the treetops and only come down to the ground occasionally, there are a few species that have reversed this arrangement, living mostly on the ground and only occasionally taking to the trees. These terrestrial monkeys have evolved larger, heavier, thickset bodies. They are generally more powerful, with huge canine teeth and strong jaws. These qualities may make them less agile in the trees, but are important as a defence mechanism when encountering trouble at ground level.

Terrestrial monkeys (baboons, geladas, drills and mandrills) are generally more powerful, with huge canine teeth, and will even take on a leopard.

The terrestrial specialists are the baboons,[3] geladas, drills and mandrills. Some of the larger macaques also spend a great deal of time on the ground, but are equally at home in the trees.

If a troop of baboons is threatened by, say, a marauding leopard, the big males will gang up on the big cat and place themselves between it and the rest of the troop. Faced with a combined threat of this sort, most leopards will give up and wander off. Occasionally they get lucky. One extraordinary incident of this kind was observed recently in which a hunting leopard managed to sneak up on a troop of baboons and kill a young one. Before it could escape with its prize, it was set upon by all the large male baboons and apparently severely injured by them. It lay on the ground and appeared to be dying. It remained there for two and a half hours, playing dead, while the baboons continued to surround it and harass it. When the baboons finally lost interest and left, the leopard calmly got up, picked up the carcass of the young one that it had killed and walked off with it to feed her cubs.[4] But this is an exceptional case. Nearly always, when faced

The slender patas monkey, the athlete of the African savannahs, capable of reaching running speeds of 34 mph (55 kph).

with a troop of angry baboons, a leopard will take fright and flee as fast as it can. In some instances, the baboons have been known to pursue a frightened leopard over long distances before abandoning the chase.

There is one terrestrial monkey that breaks the golden rule that slender monkeys should live in the trees and only heavy-weights should attempt to survive at ground level. That is the patas monkey, the athlete of the African savannahs. This animal has developed a unique survival strategy that sets it apart from all others. It has evolved very long limbs that make it the fastest monkey in the world, capable of reaching running speeds of 34 mph (55 kph). During the day the troops spend their time foraging at ground level. It is the task of the male patas to keep an eye open for trouble. He can often be seen standing up on his hind legs to peer over the tops of the long grasses. If a predator is spotted, he will threaten it with loud cries and, as he does so, will move away from the rest of the group, distracting the attacker. While he is doing this, the females will flee at top speed, eventually to be followed by the male. At night, ground level is too dangerous even for the high-speed patas, and sleeping is done in the trees, one monkey per tree, using different trees every night.

Where diet is concerned, most monkeys are opportunists that will eat almost any small food object that comes their way. A typical arboreal monkey will search for nuts, ripe fruits and berries, insects and birds' eggs. A typical ground-dweller, such as a baboon, will forage for roots, bulbs, seeds, eggs and small forms of animal life. There is, however, one branch of the monkey family that has specialized in a type of diet that the others cannot stomach. These are the leaf-eating monkeys – the colobus of Africa and the langurs of Asia. They have made the switch to a low-grade form of food that makes up for its poor nutritional value by its abundance. The only disadvantage of this kind of food is that it takes up much more of

The colobus of Africa (seen here) and the langurs of Asia are leaf-eaters.

the day simply to swallow enough to keep the animal healthy. Aiding them in their digestion is a more complex digestive system including a stomach that has several compartments. Special bacteria in the gut help to ferment the leaves and they then absorb the nutrients that are released by this fermentation process. The monkeys then in turn digest these bacteria and, in so doing, manage to retrieve these nutrients. In this way they can obtain essential proteins and ribonucleic acid.

In their social life, monkeys have two opposing considerations.[5] On the one hand, the more of them that band together the simpler it will be for them to warn one another of the presence of predators and the easier it will be to see off the predators, should it come to a showdown. Safety in numbers. On the other, the bigger the group, the less food there is to go around when they forage together. A small group, finding a cluster of tasty, ripe fruits can gorge themselves at leisure. A large group will become more edgy and competitive in case the supply runs out. And, for a very large group, there may not be enough to go round, and some members of the troop will go hungry.

It follows that every environment will suit a particular group size, and this can vary considerably even within a single species of monkey. As a result, one may see very small groups of just a few individuals, or huge packs travelling together, depending on the habitat.

Within each group there will always be a special relationship between the individuals that make it up. Everyone knows everyone else and everyone has a special status-level in relation to the others. At one extreme there is the rigid harem system of the type seen in the hamadryas baboon. Here there is a single dominant male, distinguished by his larger size and his magnificent cape of hair, surrounded by his females with their young. Typically, there are four to ten females per male. The male controls, guards and protects his females, not allowing other males near them. Unsuccessful males must hang around on the periphery in the hope that one day they may be able to acquire a few females and set up a harem of their own. If a dominant male sees one of his females wandering off, he will grab her and bite her as a punishment. Females therefore usually stay very near to their males to avoid this treatment.

Several harems may combine to form a clan. When this happens, the powerful males are usually related to one another and will have a pecking order between them based on their ages. Several of these clans may themselves combine to form a large band of up to 200 individuals. These big bands are usually only formed when the baboons are travelling or sleeping. When bands encounter one another, there may be disputes between the leading males, but sometimes the bands get together to form a large troop, perhaps sharing an ideal sleeping area.

Social life for these hamadryas baboons is clearly not a simple matter and maintaining or improving one's social status is a constant preoccupation for each adult male. For the harem females, the matter is simpler, because all they have to do is to obey their dominant male and leave matters of social status to him. His control of them is so tight that they do not even develop their own social hierarchy, with one female being dominant over another in a 'harem pecking-order'. If any female attempted to assert herself over another, she would be disciplined by the male. The only differences between females is that some of them are closer to the male than others. These are called the 'central females' and are the ones that are more socially active.

This is the most extreme form of patriarchy to be found among the monkey species. Other species of baboon are far less rigid. There, when a female comes on heat, she may mate with several of the males. The dominant ones will have preference, but the less dominant ones are not entirely excluded. They may have to wait their turn, but they will at least get a turn eventually – something that would never happen in hamadryas baboon society.

With arboreal monkeys such as guenons, the social structure is even more flexible. This is because, in the treetops, it is far more difficult for a dominant male to exert his influence on other members of his group. No sooner does he try than individuals are scampering off in one direction or another, the group dispersing and re-forming all the time. Despite this, there are usually some males who are of higher status than others and it is these the females usually seek out first when they are sexually receptive. So, although there is reproductive hope for most males, it is the most socially impressive ones that have the best chance of producing offspring.

With all monkeys
a single offspring is
usually produced,
but there may
occasionally be
twins.

A special case, where the males went too far in the dominance battle, concerns the patas monkey of the African grasslands. This ground-dwelling species lives in uni-male groups, but the size of the typical female harem is too big for the male to dominate it. If he tries to assert himself, the females gang up on him and become the group controllers. They are so assertive that most of the squabbling you see in a patas group is not between males but between the dominant females who are trying to sort out their social hierarchy. So the male's main task is watching out for predators and protecting his group of females from danger, rather than dominating them socially. He has become their sexual servant, allowed to mate with them when the time comes, but otherwise of no social importance within the group. The patas monkey is an intriguing example of a patriarchy that went so far it became a matriarchy.

When the young are born, the pattern of behaviour is much the same with all species of monkey. A single offspring is usually produced. Monkey twins are rarer than human twins, but do sometimes occur. The big difference between a monkey baby and a human baby is that the young monkey is capable of clinging on to the mother from birth. This is because the newborn monkey's arms are stronger at birth and because the mother's fur provides a better grip for the tiny fingers. At one closely observed monkey birth it was possible to see that the baby was actually aiding its own delivery by grasping hold of its mother's fur while it was emerging from her body.[6]

Once born, the infant monkey will spend some weeks clinging tightly to its mother's body as she moves around. Even if she should have to flee in panic, the little one will still be able to hang on and avoid being dislodged, despite the violent movements it must endure.

As times passes, the young monkey will start to explore near its mother when she is resting, but it will keep a constant eye on her and she on it. At the slightest sign of trouble, she will scoop it up or it will run to her and cling on to her fur again. These times spent away from the mother's body will gradually increase and the young monkey will start to meet up with others of its own age. Vigorous play then becomes a common occurrence as the young grow and become stronger. Compared with other animals, this period of childhood is lengthy and in a typical monkey it will take four to five years before adulthood has been reached.

10 Unusual Monkeys

PROBOSCIS MONKEY

The monkey with the strangest nose is undoubtedly the proboscis monkey from Borneo. It is known locally as the *monyet belanda*, which translates as 'Dutch monkey' – because the locals thought that it reminded them of the early Dutch travellers they met, who apparently also had large noses and big bellies.

The proboscis monkey always lives near water and some of it toes are webbed. It is the most aquatic of all monkeys and is an excellent swimmer, being able to remain submerged for at least 20 m (65 ft). Its most unusual feature, however, is the huge, pendulous nose of the adult male that can grow to a length of 18 cm (7 in.).

The function of this bulbous appendage is still debated. Some see it as a visual display of male dominance, with the biggest nose having the greatest sex appeal for the females. Others see it as aiding in the very loud *kee-honk* noise made by the adult males as an alarm call. When the males sense a threat, blood rushes to the nose and engorges it so that it swells out even more and becomes a resonating cavity, enhancing the impact of the hooting cries that are used to alert the other members of the group to the presence of danger.

In reality the great nose probably functions in both these ways, attracting females and signalling danger. It gives this species a bizarre, unique appearance that makes it impossible to confuse it with any of the other 172 species of monkey.

The monkey with the strangest nose is the proboscis monkey from Borneo. The huge, pendulous nose of the adult male can grow to a length of 7 inches.

Another Asiatic monkey with an odd nasal arrangement is the snub-nosed monkey. Here the nose is the exact opposite of the one seen on the proboscis monkey. That one is huge while this one is virtually non-existent. All that is left is a pair of small nasal holes – upturned nostrils that have the unfortunate habit of collecting raindrops and making the monkeys sneeze in wet weather.

Altogether there are eight species of these monkeys, living at relatively high altitudes across a wide range in Southeast Asia from Burma, Cambodia and Laos to Vietnam and southern China. Although they have very different markings, they all have in common the same, curious little upturned nose. It has been suggested that the extreme flattening of the nose is a device to combat extreme cold and to avoid the frostbite that might damage a more fleshy nasal appendage. This does not seem very convincing. A heavier, more protruding nose could contain complex air passages that would warm the cold air as it passed through and before it reached the delicate lining of the lungs.

Whatever the true function of these curious nostrils, they, along with bright facial colour patches, do give these monkeys one of the strangest and most unforgettable of all primate faces.

JAPANESE MACAQUE

The snub-nosed monkey. Its nose and the bright facial colour patches give these monkeys the strangest of all primates' faces.

The most northern of all the monkeys, the Japanese macaque, is capable of living in regions that are too cold for any other species. It is able to cope with temperatures as low as -20°C (-4°F). Despite the huge human population in Japan, there are still more than 100,000 of these tough macaques living in that country today.

Appropriately known as the 'snow monkey', its hair is so thick that it looks as though it is wearing a fur coat over its ordinary fur.

The most northern of all the monkeys, the Japanese macaque is capable of living in regions that are too cold for any other species. As a respite from the snow, it enjoys the warmth of hot springs in the Nagano region of Japan.

Its short tail is also densely furred and the only part of its body that is exposed to the low temperatures is its red-skinned face. It appears to keep this area uncovered because its changing facial expressions are an important part of social communication.

This species became famous for the photographs showing it enjoying the warmth of an open-air hot spring near a ski resort in the Nagano region of Japan. The land around the hot spring was covered in snow and some of the monkeys, up to their necks in the warm water, still had snow on the hairs on the tops of their heads.

In this region the land is covered in snow for four months of the year and it is hard to see how the Japanese macaques in this area are able to survive. It was only recently that they began using the hot springs to keep warm. In 1963 some of the more adventurous ones descended from the steep, forested cliffs nearby, sensed the warmth coming from the steamy water and climbed in. Soon they were joined by others until it became a regular habit to spend all day in the luxury of the springs. When dusk fell each evening, they would climb out, spend the night in the security of the forest trees and then return again the next morning. The agonizing moment when they have to get out into the freezing air with soaking wet fur does not bear thinking about. It is a wonder that they do not freeze solid inside a block of ice.

11 Rare Monkeys

Primate conservationists and field-workers have been working globally to halt the widespread decline in monkey numbers, but they are facing an almost impossible task and, to be brutally honest, their attempts so far have largely failed. This is not surprising when one considers the habitats occupied by most monkeys. Confined largely to the tropics, they occupy regions where there is widespread human poverty and cultural instability.

In such places it is difficult to convince the local people that monkey survival is important when they can barely control their own survival. To them the very concept of animal conservation is an elitist Western conceit, with echoes of old-fashioned colonialism. If their children are in desperate need of animal protein and monkey meat tastes good, then hunting will flourish, whatever the law says.

If the West is desperate for more and more wood to convert into the newspapers, magazines, books, cardboard boxes and the sheets of paper that seems to saturate the daily life of the more advanced societies, then out come the deadly chainsaws and down come the monkeys' precious trees, felled not with any sense of ecological shame, but rather with unabashed pride.

If human populations start to explode – and they are doing this most acutely in just those regions favoured by wild monkey species, then the spread of agriculture and the growth of urban

Capuchin monkeys (*Cebus apella*) cooked for meat, Boca Mishagua River, Amazonià, Peru.

centres will soon gobble up more and more of the wild places. And if someone should find oil or some other valuable natural resource lurking below the surface of some remote, monkey-rich location, then, of course, nothing is allowed to stand in the way of wholesale habitat destruction and modern industrial progress.

Bearing all this in mind, it is hardly surprising that primate conservation is largely a matter of making careful field observations, reporting back to HQ, drawing up meticulous lists, re-classifying a few sub-species, and then issuing dire warnings that go unheeded.

The monkey populations, meanwhile, continue to decline at a frightening rate. Of the 173 species now recognized, twenty of them are so critically endangered that they will probably not survive the present century. Their details are given overleaf:

SPECIES	FORMAL NAME	LOCATION	POPULATION
Blond capuchin	*Cebus flavius*	E. Brazil	180
Yellow-breasted capuchin	*Cebus xanthosternos*	Brazil	Unknown
Variegated spider monkey	*Ateles hybridus*	Colombia, Venezuela	Unknown
Northern woolly spider monkey	*Brachyteles hypoxanthus*	Brazil	855
Yellow-tailed woolly monkey	*Oreonax flavicauda*	Peru	Unknown
Arunachal macaque	*Macaca munzala*	N.E. India	250–569
Sanjei mangabey	*Cercocebus sanjei*	Tanzania	Fewer than 1,300
Highland mangabey	*Rungwecebus kipunji*	Tanzania	1,100
Drill	*Mandrillus leucophaeus*	W. Africa	Unknown
Sclater's monkey	*Cercopithecus sclateri*	Nigeria	Unknown

The drill, the only close relative of the mandrill, is now down to a population of little more than 3,000 in its West African home.

The population of the yellow-tailed woolly monkey of Peru (*Oreonax flavicauda*) is down to just a few hundred and its future looks bleak.

SPECIES	FORMAL NAME	LOCATION	POPULATION
Pennant's colobus	*Procolobus pennantii*	W. Africa	Unknown
Tana river red colobus	*Piliocolobus rufomitratus*	Kenya	Fewer than 1,000
Niger Delta red colobus	*Procolobus epeini*	Nigeria	Unknown
Delacour's langur	*Trachypithecus delacouri*	Vietnam	200 or fewer
Pig-tailed langur	*Simias concolor*	Mentawi Islands	3,347
Grey-shanked douc	*Pygathrix cinerea*	Vietnam	600–700
Tonkin snub-nosed monkey	*Rhinopithecus avunculus*	Vietnam	Fewer than 200
Black snub-nosed monkey	*Rhinopithecus bieti*	China	Fewer than 2,000
Grey snub-nosed monkey	*Rhinopithecus brelichi*	China	Around 750
Burmese snub-nosed monkey	*Rhinopithecus strykeri*	Burma	300

There are fewer than 2,000 black snub-nosed monkeys (*Rhinopithecus bieti*) left in the wild in China.

The Tonkin snub-nosed monkey (*Rhinopithecus avunculus*) of Vietnam is one of the rarest of all monkeys, with a tiny surviving population of less than 200.

12 Newly Discovered Monkeys

It is extremely rare for a new species of large mammal to be found today, so it is surprising to learn that no fewer than six new species of monkey have been discovered in the last few years – a guenon, a macaque, a mangabey, a capuchin, a colobus and a snub-nosed monkey. The reason for this is that, despite the depredations of logging, there remain vast tracts of dense forest that are difficult for explorers to penetrate. If a species of monkey has become isolated in a small patch of forest it can remain undetected for years, even if there is fieldwork being carried out in the region. This is what appears to have happened in these recent cases.

THE SUN-TAILED MONKEY

The first of these new monkeys was found in Africa in 1984 and was not scientifically described until 1988. It has been given the name of sun-tailed monkey, or sun-tailed guenon, and the scientific name of *Cercopithecus solatus*. It lives in one hilly area of the moist evergreen forests of Gabon in West Africa, preferring the densely shaded, tangled areas. Its small population appears to have been hemmed in by four local rivers that act as boundaries restricting its spread. Primarily a fruit-eater, it spends its time partly in the trees and partly on the ground, moving about in small troops each consisting of one male and a number of females with their young. At night the troops retreat to the forest canopy to sleep.

Spending so much time at ground level, it has become a stealthy species and lacks any loud cries that could give away its presence. There are no long-distance calls or high-pitched contact calls, although the males do perform a warning bark when alarmed.

The sun-tailed monkey should not be confused with the red-tailed monkey. In the sun-tailed species the long tail is light grey except for its tip that is orange-red. In the red-tailed monkey the tail is orange-red down most of its length.

In 1996 the Republic of Gabon honoured this new discovery by placing its image on their 500F postage stamp.

The sun-tailed monkey (*Cercopithecus solatus*) was not scientifically described until 1988. It lives in one hilly area of the moist evergreen forests of Gabon in West Africa. The long tail is light grey except for its tip, which is orange-red.

When it was first discovered in 1993, this new monkey was thought to be no more than a local variant, but in 2007 it was elevated to the rank of a full species and in 2010 it was included in the shortlist of the most critically endangered of all primate species.

Restricted to the marsh forest zone of the central delta, its hopes of survival in the future are slender indeed. The region is plagued by political unrest, bushmeat hunting, canal building, and logging, including the destruction its favourite food-trees. As a result, with its numbers already low, it will probably soon become extinct, despite the best efforts by conservationists to save it. It has been estimated that, during the past 30 years, its population size has shrunk by as much as 80 per cent.

It is a species with distinctive markings. The upper surface, from head to rump, is black. The sides and outer legs are orange-brown; the inner legs, the underside and most of the arms are white, while the hands and feet are black. The tail is a reddish brown on top and maroon underneath, getting darker towards the tip. On its otherwise dark face there are conspicuous white sideburns.

THE ARUNACHAL MACAQUE

Moving into the twenty-first century, in 2003 a new species of macaque was discovered in a poorly explored, remote district of northeast India by a team of biologists from the Nature Conservation Foundation. This region is known as the Arunachal Pradesh. It is an area of rugged mountains with extensive forest cover and has been described as 'one of the last truly wild places of India'.

The team of explorers were investigating the high altitude regions of this northeastern-most tip of India when they came across what must be one of the highest living of all primates,

A Discovered in 1993, the Niger Delta red colobus monkey was elevated to the rank of a full species in 2007. Its hopes of survival in the future are slender because the region is plagued by political unrest, hunting and logging.

In 2003 a new species of monkey, the Arunachal macaque, was discovered in a remote district of northeast India. It was the first new macaque species to be recorded for over a century.

occupying an environmental niche between 2,000 and 3,500 m (6,650 and 11,400 ft). Given the name of Arunachal macaque (*Macaca munzala*), it resembled other, more common species of macaque, but it was claimed that this similarity was the result of convergent evolution rather than close affinity. Genetically, it is believed to be a distinct species and not merely a local race, as has been claimed by some authorities. When its details were published a few years later, in 2006, it was the first new macaque species to be recorded for more than 100 years. In that same year an additional population was discovered just over the border in Bhutan.

The species name *munzala* means 'deep forest monkey' in the dialect of the local inhabitants. The Arunachal macaque is a compact-bodied animal with pink 'spectacles' surrounded by a dark face. It has an orange-buff crown-patch with a dark wedge through it, a prognathous skull, a prominent ruff that changes colour with the seasons, becoming paler in December, a dense white underside and a short tail.

Recently it has been seen raiding crops in the region and has, inevitably, been persecuted by local farmers as a result. Its long-term future, like that of so many monkey species, is therefore at risk.

THE KIPUNJI

The discovery as recently as 2004 of a completely new species in Tanzania, so distinct that it had to be given its own genus, came as a shock to those involved. An IUCN spokesman summed up the surprise felt when he declared: 'A large, striking monkey in a country of considerable wildlife research over the last century has been hidden right under our noses.'

Even more bizarre is the fact that it was simultaneously dis-covered by two independent teams of fieldworkers approaching

The kipunji, a completely new species of monkey, discovered in Tanzania in 2004.

its forest home from two different directions.[1] When they found out about one another, although probably disappointed at having to share their exciting discovery, they nevertheless combined forces to make an official report on the new species. As one of the fieldworkers said: 'These monkeys have probably been there for hundreds of thousands of years. What are the chances of two independent projects finding the animal within a ten-month period?'

An East African monkey, the kipunji inhabits a small area in the forests of the southern highlands of Tanzania. There are estimated to be no more than 1,100 of them in existence, living in a region where illegal logging is causing great damage to the habitat. Consequently, their future looks bleak.

The kipunji is an arboreal species, living in mountainside trees. It is brown in colour with an off-white belly and tail, an erect crest on its head, long cheek whiskers and a black face. A special feature is its distinctive territorial call: a low-pitched 'honk-bark' that it shares with no other species. The calls of its nearest relatives have been described as something very different – as 'whoop-gobbles'.

The thick coat of the kipunji adapts it well to the altitude where it lives – as high as 2,450 m (8,000 ft) – where the nights can be very cold. In 2005 it was given the scientific name of *Rungwecebus kipunji*: *Rungwecebus* because it lives on Mount Rungwe and *kipunji* because that is the name used to describe it by local tribes.

THE BLOND CAPUCHIN

In 2006 a pale-coloured capuchin monkey, long thought to be extinct, was rediscovered in the coastal forests of Eastern Brazil. One of the rarest primates on the planet, it is believed that the world population of blond capuchins totals no more than 180.

The species was first noted as far back as 1648 and again in 1774, but then virtually vanished from sight and there was no specimen to confirm its existence, let alone its survival. It was not fully documented until 2006, when it was rediscovered in the forests along the Atlantic coast of Brazil.

Its coat is a uniformly pale golden colour with a whitish cap on its head and a pinkish face. The palms of its hands and feet are black.

In their behaviour, blond capuchins demonstrate tool-using on a par with that of Africa's chimpanzees. Field observations have revealed that when a group of them came across a termite hill, several of the males in the group would start hitting the hill with their hands. They then selected thin branches and poked these into the hill using a rotation insertion technique to gain entry. After probing with their sticks, they then withdrew them, inspected them closely and ate any termites clinging there. Still holding on to their implements, they would then tap the hill

In 2006 the blond capuchin was rediscovered in the coastal forests of eastern Brazil.

again with their free hand and repeat the procedure. This feeding method marks the blond capuchin out as one of the most intelligent of all living monkeys. Human fieldworkers found that, if they imitated the monkey's technique of tapping the termite hill and then rotating the twig when inserting it, they too were able to obtain a better catch than if they omitted these actions.

THE BURMESE SNUB-NOSED MONKEY

The latest monkey find, the Burmese snub-nosed monkey (*Rhinopthecus strykeri*), was discovered in Myanmar as recently as 2010. At first it was known only from skin and skulls obtained from local

The Burmese snub-nosed monkey was discovered in Myanmar in 2010. The population is small, only about 300 individuals, living in a mountainous area hemmed in by two large rivers.

hunters, who hunt it for its meat. Local people in the north-eastern Burmese state of Kachin spoke of a monkey they knew as *mey nwoah*, meaning 'monkey with an upturned face', but scientists had yet to set eyes upon it.

Snub-nosed monkeys were previously only known from China, Laos, Cambodia and Vietnam, so the search was on for this elusive species. The hunters offered a useful tip: search for this particular monkey when it is raining because the rainwater gets into their upturned nostrils and makes them sneeze. They sneeze so loudly that it is easy to track them down. When they get fed up with sneezing, they sit down with their heads tucked between their knees, waiting for the rain to stop. When it is not raining, the hunters said, the monkey is extremely difficult to find because it is so quiet.

When it was finally located by the scientists, it emerged that the population was amazingly small – only about 300 individuals – living in a mountainous area hemmed in by two large rivers. Isolated in this way, the monkey had slowly evolved into a distinct species, with black body and legs, white ear-tufts and white beards, prominent lips, wide upturned nostrils, bare pink faces and a black tail longer than its body. It was a dramatically large animal, bigger than any previously known snub-nosed monkeys.

Nicknamed 'Snubby' by its discoverers, this monkey is clearly on the verge of extinction. It is hoped to make the local people so proud of their unique animal that they stop hunting it to oblivion simply for its meat, but this may not be easy. It also has to contend with a planned dam construction, illegal logging in the region, and the persistent demand for exotic forms of Chinese medicine.

13 Intelligent Monkeys

During earlier centuries the monkey has occasionally been spared its humiliating symbolic role of a meddling, evil clown, and been allowed to represent a quality that does at least bear some relation to its natural self – its cleverness. One of the earliest of the legendary 'clever monkeys' was one called Bertrand who, wanting some chestnuts roasting in the fire, used a cat's paw to obtain them.[1] The cat complained of the pain, but was told by the monkey that the prize would be shared between them, a promise that it failed to keep. The fable of the cat's paw became famous and was repeated time and again down the centuries, but although it showed how intelligent the monkey was in relation to another animal, it still cast the monkey in the unpleasant role of a trickster.

Another early reference to the monkey's intelligence appeared in *The Book of Wisdom* in 1483, where a group of six monkeys are endeavouring to catch birds. To help them with this, they are collecting sticks to start a fire that will smoke the birds out of a hollow tree. It is strange to see tool-using monkeys depicted in this way as long ago as the fifteenth century, because the fact that they do, indeed, use tools in the wild has been a comparatively recent discovery.

Turning from these early images to the real animals, it is true to say that all monkeys are bright, but some are more intelligent

Six clever monkeys in *The Book of Wisdom* (1483). This was one of the earliest books to be printed by the Gutenberg press.

than others. The sage of the monkey world is undoubtedly the small capuchin monkey from Central and South America. This species not only learns extremely complicated tricks in captivity, but also performs extraordinary feats in the wild.[2]

One of the most amazing animal videos of all time shows a capuchin monkey opening a hard palm-nut using a large rock as a tool. The animal begins by selecting a fallen log that has a small depression in its upper surface. It bangs the nut against this log

In the wild the small capuchin is capable of opening a hard palm-nut by hammering it with a heavy stone weighing up to 77 per cent of its own body weight. A similar tool-using ability has been observed in chimpanzees, but in no other monkeys.

four times and then places it in the depression so that it does not roll off. It then finds a large, smooth rock, so heavy the monkey can barely lift it, and carries it with difficulty to the log. Once there, it stands on its hind legs, raises the rock above its head in both hands and brings it crashing down on the nut.

The aim is perfect but the nut is too hard and refuses to break. It takes the persistent animal three minutes of energetic hammering to open the nut. In all, it makes nineteen blows with its large rock and between each of the blows, picks up the nut, taps it a few times on the log to see if it has started cracking open, then places it back in the small depression and gives it another massive blow with the rock. Once it senses that the nut is weakening, it rains blow after blow on it without bothering to examine it between hits. At last the nut cracks open and the monkey quickly scampers up a tree to devour its contents.

This is tool-using on a level that even a chimpanzee would find hard to match. The combination of careful anvil selection, heavy weightlifting, accurate aiming, crack-testing and, above all, remarkable persistence of a kind rarely seen in human children faced with similar tasks, make the capuchin one of the brainiest of all non-human animals. Little wonder that this is the species that is always employed when companion animals for the disabled are being trained.

On one occasion, field-workers tested the intelligence of wild capuchins by experimentally giving them a choice of 'hammers'. They offered hard stones versus crumbly stones, light stones versus heavy stones, and large stones versus small stones. In every case, the monkeys tested the different objects and then chose the one that was hard enough, heavy enough and large enough to crack open the palm nuts. In a total of 377 tests, they only failed to open the nut on 39 occasions – almost a 90 per cent success rate.

The 'hammer' rocks are nearly always smooth, like large pebbles, and it was discovered that these had to be carried quite a distance to the site where they were used on the log-anvils. Even more extraordinary is the fact that, when tested, it was found that one rock weighed 77 per cent of the body weight of the monkey that carried and it and then used it.

The only drawback to using these highly intelligent ways of obtaining food is that the actions involved are noisy and the repeated banging of the rocks can sometimes attract a predator. But the brainy capuchins even have an answer for this eventuality. If they are disturbed by a jaguar, for example, they rapidly

Bertrand and the cat's paw. Marcus Gheeraerts illustrates the ancient fable of the monkey and the cat, where the clever monkey uses the cat's paw to scoop chestnuts from the hot fire.

climb to the top of a rocky escarpment, or a cliff, where they find a new use for loose rocks, hurling them down onto the big cat below until it beats a hasty retreat.

Wild capuchins have also been observed to use tools for digging in the forest floor for tubers. Tubers are a particularly nutritious source of food but are not easy to excavate from the hard earth. The capuchins solve this problem by finding a suitable stone, holding it in one hand and banging it down on the surface several times in quick succession. This has the effect of loosening the hard soil and, as the monkey hammers away with one hand, it simultaneously scoops the softened patch of earth away with the other. In this way it can dig deeper and deeper until it finds its buried treasure.

In captivity, given art materials, capuchins have been known to make drawings with fan-shaped patterns similar to those made by chimpanzees.

In addition to cracking open hard nuts and digging for tubers, capuchins have also been observed using sticks to probe into crevices in trees and rock faces, prising out small, hidden food objects. Some capuchins have also been seen fishing for termites with small sticks, a tool-using feat that was previously thought to be the sole preserve of the wild chimpanzee.

All these tool-using activities increase when the environment fails to deliver easy meals, and may disappear altogether during periods of lush plenty. For capuchins, as with humans, necessity is the mother of invention.

In the laboratory many subtle tests have been carried out with capuchins and their level of intelligence has never ceased to surprise the experimenters. To give one example: two capuchins were separated by a glass screen with a small hole in it. One capuchin had a stone hammer and the other a jar full of nuts that he could not open. The first capuchin passed the hammer through the hole in the glass partition and the second one used it to knock open the lid of the jar. When he had extracted the nuts from inside the jar, instead of eating them all himself, he shared them with his helpful companion.

In another laboratory test, one capuchin was given a small biscuit as a reward whenever he offered the experimenter a small token. He happily ate the biscuit until he noticed that his companion monkey was getting a succulent grape as a reward instead of a dry biscuit. After this, he would hand over a token and, if given another biscuit, would throw it away angrily and keep trying until eventually he obtained a grape.

These two tests reveal that capuchins have both a sense of mutual aid and cooperation, and a sense of fairness and unfairness. One can't help thinking that, if they could talk, we would have to open an embassy for them.

Timeline of the Monkey

34 MILLION BC	30 MILLION BC	c. 2400 BC	13TH CENTURY AD
Monkeys evolve from prosimians	African monkeys migrate to South America	Egyptians tame baboons as pets and depict them being walked on leads	Monkeys presented as debauched, ugly and hateful in medieval bestiaries

1642	1658	1774	c. 1800
Prince Rupert of the Rhine is satirically ridiculed about his famous pet monkey	Topsel's *History of Four-footed Beasts* describes nine kinds of monkeys	Stubbs's *Portrait of a Monkey* shows the animal picking a peach	In the Napoleonic Wars, the English hang a ship-wrecked monkey as a French spy

1949	1953	1979	1981
A rhesus monkey is the first monkey rocketed into space	The first volume of Osman Hill's eight-volume study of primates is published	A capuchin is the first money to operate as a service animal	In *Raiders of the Lost Ark*, a capuchin monkey plays a Nazi spy

1560	1562	17TH CENTURY AD
Gesner recognizes only four species of monkeys in *Icones Animalium*	Peter Bruegel creates one of the first paintings with monkeys as its central feature	The Three Wise Monkeys appear in a carving in Nikkō, Japan

1871	1912	1925	1942
Darwin's *The Descent of Man* presents evidence supporting common ancestry	Daniel Elliot's *A Review of the Primates* is published	The infamous Scopes Monkey Trial takes place	Churchill orders reinforcements for the Barbary macaques of Gibraltar

1999	2003	2010
The first cloned monkey is born at the Oregon Primate Research Center	The Arunachal macaque discovered in northeastern India	The Burmese snub-nosed monkey discovered in Myanmar

Appendix 1:
Classification

When Gesner set out his rather primitive classification of animals in his *Icones Animalium* of 1560, he recognized only four kinds of monkeys.[1] The first is what we now know as the Barbary macaque from North Africa. This is accurately illustrated as a tailless monkey and was in those days generally referred to as an ape. The accuracy of the illustration, showing an animal that is not yet fully grown, suggests that the drawing was done from a live specimen kept as a pet.

Second is the baboon, depicted in what looks like a posture of prayer, but is probably meant to represent begging for food. A sad creature, with a huge mane of hair and a large sexual swelling, it squats on the ground, looking emaciated and thoroughly miserable. When African baboons reached Europe at this early date, they were probably not in the best of condition.

Third, there is a remarkably well-drawn portrayal of a guenon monkey from West Africa. Tethered by a chain and waist-belt to a ring in the ground, this animal is alert and well proportioned, and was presumably a well-cared for pet.

Finally, and in complete contrast, there is a flight of fancy called a 'satyr' in the shape of a bipedal creature with a naked body and a mane of hair all around its head. Clearly a female, it has breasts and a hint of a sexual swelling. It also has a very long tail and is carrying a walking stick. Unsurprisingly, it is described

In Gesner's primitive classification of animals in his *Icones Animalium* of 1560, he recognizes only four kinds of monkeys. The first is what we now know as the Barbary macaque from North Africa.

as 'rare'. To be more precise, he described it as 'a rare cercopithecus of human size and shape' (*'formae rarae Cercopithecus, magnitudine & forma hominis'*).

Such was Gesner's authority that this fictitious creature was faithfully copied and described in later volumes of natural history for at least 200 years. What could it have been? Was it entirely imaginary, or was it based on a real monkey of some kind? It seems that he borrowed the illustration from a travel book by Bernhard von Breydenbach that records a visit made by the author to the Holy Land. While there, he may have observed, or been told about, hamadryas baboons with their impressive manes of hair, and created an imaginative version of them that Gesner then enshrined in the early zoological literature.

The first description we have in English of this mysterious satyr monkey appears in Topsel's *History of Four-footed Beasts*. In the 1658 version of his work, he comments as follows:

There is another kind of Munkey, for stature, bignesse and shape like a man, for by his knees, secret parts and face, you

175

would judge him a wild man, such as inhabit *Numidia,* and the *Lapones,* for he is altogether overgrown with hair; no creature, except a man can stand as long as he; he loveth women and children dearly, like other of his own kind, and is so venereous that he will attempt to ravish women, whose image is here described, as it was taken forth of the book of the description of the Holy Land.[2]

This is clearly a creature of fantasy based on wild tales with confused origins, but was probably based on the hamadryas baboon. Being little known, it was exaggerated by traveller's tales into a raping monster.

In addition to the satyr, Topsel lists eight others kinds of primates. Although they are given strange names, they appear to be based on the following: 1 Barbary macaque (Topsel's *Ape*); 2 Guenon (Topsel's *Munkey*); 3 Capuchin (Topsel's *Martine Munkey*); 4 Lion-tailed macaque (Topsel's *Bearded Ape*); 5 Langur (Topsel's *Prasyan Ape)*; 6 Unnamed (Topsel's *Munkey . . . like a man*); 7 Common baboon (Topsel's *Baboun*); 8 Hamadryas baboon (Topsel's *Tartarine*).

This collection reveals that, by the middle of the seventeenth century, a few new species are becoming known in Europe. However, it will not be until towards the end of the nineteenth century that hordes of Victorian explorers will have collected specimens of many different kinds of monkeys. The rise in numbers is dramatic. In his 1806 survey of known monkeys, Forbes is able to list no fewer than 118 Old World monkeys and 31 New World monkeys, a total of 149 different kinds.[3]

So the classification of monkeys leapt from four in the sixteenth century to nine in the seventeenth century, to 149 in the nineteenth century. By the end of the twentieth century, this number had decreased to a total of 102 because, although a few new species were added, many of the old ones had been discarded as representing no more than local variations.[4]

In the twenty-first century, this has changed again with the latest officially accepted list recording as many as 173 species.[5] This dramatic new increase is due to three factors. The first is that a few

Gesner's 1560 baboon is depicted in what looks like a posture of prayer, but is probably begging for food. A sad creature, with a huge mane of hair and a large sexual swelling.

new species have been discovered. The second is that a great deal of new field-work has been carried out making it possible to identify genuinely separate species that were previously thought to be no more than local variants. The third, sadly, is that some field-workers and conservationists are unduly biased in favour of elevating local variants to the level of full species because this makes the animals in question appear more important and therefore more in need of protection.

As a result, there is still a great deal of debate as to exactly how many true species should be recognized. The academic battle between the 'lumpers', usually museum-based authorities, and the 'splitters', usually field-workers, continues.

The lumpers are generally only fully satisfied when two species overlap in the wild without interbreeding, or if they are so dramatically different in appearance from one another that their separation into different species cannot be denied.

The splitters argue that if the museum men would go into the field they would see for themselves that many local variants are often so different in the way they live that they must be given the status of different species. As the two sides will probably never agree, the strategy adopted here, to provide a useful working list of monkey species, is to show the main species accepted by both the lumpers and the splitters in **heavy type** and those only accepted by the splitters in ordinary type. In this way, both camps can be satisfied. The new species, discovered in the past few years, are shown in ***bold italics.***

It should be mentioned that, with the New World primates, the smaller species such as the marmosets, tamarins, and their relatives are beyond the scope of this book and are excluded. Only the larger, more typical monkeys – the capuchins, squirrel monkeys, howlers, spider monkeys and woolly monkeys – from that region are listed here, along with all the Old World monkeys.

MONKEY CLASSIFICATION SUMMARY

Capuchin monkeys	9	South and Central America
Squirrel monkeys	5	South and Central America
Howler monkeys	10	South and Central America
Spider monkeys	9	South and Central America
Woolly monkeys	5	South America
Macaques	21	Asia and North Africa
Mangabeys	9	Africa
Kipunji	1	Africa
Baboons	5	Africa
Drills	2	Africa
Gelada	1	Africa
Guenons	31	Africa
Talapoin	2	Africa
Allen's swamp monkey	1	Africa
Patas monkey	1	Africa
Colobus	16	Asia
Proboscis monkey	1	Asia
Leaf monkeys	36	Asia
Snub-nosed monkeys	8	Asia

MONKEY SPECIES CLASSIFICATION (173 SPECIES)

NEW WORLD MONKEYS (38 SPECIES)

CAPUCHINS

White-fronted capuchin	*Cebus albifrons*	South America
Tufted or Brown capuchin	*Cebus apella*	South America
White-faced capuchin	*Cebus capucinus*	Central and South America
Blond capuchin	*Cebus flavius*	E. Brazil
Kaapori capuchin	*Cebus kaapori*	N. Brazil
Black-striped capuchin	*Cebus libidinosus*	Brazil
Black capuchin	*Cebus nigritis*	S. Brazil
Weeper capuchin	*Cebus olivaceus*	N. South America
Yellow-breasted capuchin	*Cebus xanthosternos*	E. Brazil

SQUIRREL MONKEYS

Black-capped squirrel monkey	*Saimiri boliviensis*	South America
Central American squirrel monkey	*Saimiri oerstedi*	Central America
Common squirrel monkey	*Saimiri sciureus*	South America
Bare-eared squirrel monkey	*Saimiri ustus*	Central South America
Black squirrel monkey	*Saimiri vanzolinii*	N.W. Brazil

HOWLER MONKEYS

Red-handed howler monkey	*Alouatta belzebul*	N. Brazil
Black howler monkey	*Alouatta caraya*	South America
Coiba Island howler monkey	*Alouatta coibensis*	Panama
Brown howler monkey	*Alouatta guariba*	S.E. Brazil
Guyanan howler monkey	*Alouatta macconnelli*	N. South America
Amazon black howler	*Alouatta nigerrima*	Central Brazil
Mantled howler monkey	*Alouatta palliata*	Central and South America
Guatemalan howler monkey	*Alouatta pigra*	Central America
Bolivian red howler	*Alouatta sara*	Bolivia
Red howler monkey	*Alouatta seniculus*	N.W. South America

SPIDER MONKEYS

Long-haired spider monkey	*Ateles belzebuth*	N. South America
Peruvian spider monkey	*Ateles chamek*	South America
Brown-headed spider monkey	*Ateles fusciceps*	Central and South America
Black-handed spider monkey	*Ateles geoffroyi*	Central America
Variegated spider monkey	*Ateles hybridus*	N. South America
White-cheeked spider monkey	*Ateles marginatus*	Central Brazil
Black spider monkey	*Ateles paniscus*	E. South America
Southern woolly spider monkey	*Brachyteles arachnoids*	S.E. Brazil
Northern woolly spider monkey	*Brachyteles hypoxanthus*	E. Brazil

WOOLLY MONKEYS

Grey woolly monkey	*Lagothrix cana*	South America
Humboldt's woolly monkey	*Lagothrix lagotricha*	South America
Colombian woolly monkey	*Lagothrix lugens*	Colombia
Silvery woolly wonkey	*Lagothrix poeppigii*	W. South America
Yellow-tailed woolly monkey	*Oreonax flavicauda*	South America

OLD WORLD MONKEYS (134 SPECIES)

Stump-tailed macaque	*Macaca arctoides*	S. Asia
Assamese macaque	*Macaca assamensis*	S. Asia
Formosan macaque	*Macaca cyclopis*	Taiwan
Crab-eating macaque	*Macaca fasicularis*	S. Asia, Sumatra, Java, Borneo and Philippines
Japanese macaque	*Macaca fuscata*	Japan
Heck's macaque	*Macaca hecki*	N. Sulawesi
Northern pig-tailed macaque	*Macaca leonine*	S. Asia
Moor macaque	*Macaca maura*	S. Sulawesi
Rhesus macaque	*Macaca mulatta*	S. Asia
*Arunachal macaqu*e	*Macaca munzala*	N.E. India
Southern pig-tailed macaque	*Macaca nemestrina*	S. Asia, Sumatra, Borneo
Celebes crested macaque	*Macaca nigra*	N.E. Sulawesi
Gorongalo macaque	*Macaca nigrescens*	N. Sulawesi
Booted macaque	*Macaca ochreata*	S.E. Sulawesi
Bonnet macaque	*Macaca radiata*	S. Asia
Siberut macaque	Macaca siberu	Siberut Island, off Sumatra
Lion-tailed macaque	*Macaca silenus*	S. Asia
Toque macaque	*Macaca sinica*	Sri Lanka
Barbary macaque	*Macaca sylvanus*	N. Africa
Pere David's macaque	*Macaca thibetana*	China
Tonkean macaque	*Macaca tonkeana*	Central and N. Sulawesi

Agile mangabey	*Cercocebus agilis*	Central Africa
Sooty mangabey	*Cercocebus atys*	Central W. Africa
Golden-bellied mangabey	*Cercocebus chrysogaster*	Central Africa
Tana River mangabey	*Cercocebus galeritus*	E. Africa
Sanje manabey	*Cercocebus sanjei*	Central E. Africa
Collared mangabey	*Cercocebus torquatus*	Central W. Africa
Grey-cheeked mangabey	*Lophocebus albigena*	Central Africa
Black-crested mangabey	*Lophocebus aterrimus*	Central Africa
Opdenbosch's mangabey	*Lophocebus opdenboschi*	Dem. Rep. Congo

Kipunji	*Rungwecebus kipunji*	Tanzania

BABOONS

Olive or Anubis baboon	*Papio anubis*	Central Africa
Yellow baboon	*Papio cynocephalus*	E. Africa
Hamadryas baboon	*Papio hamadryas*	N. E. Africa and S. W. Asia
Guinea baboon	*Papio papio*	W. Africa
Chacma baboon	*Papio ursinus*	S. Africa

DRILLS

Drill	*Mandrillus leucophaeus*	W. Africa
Mandrill	*Mandrillus sphinx*	W. Africa

GELADA

Gelada	*Theropithecus gelada*	N. E. Africa

GUENONS

Samango or Syke's monkey	*Cercopithecus albogularis*	Tropical Africa
Redtail and Coppertail monkey	*Cercopithecus ascanius*	Central Africa
Campbell's monkey	*Cercopithecus campbelli*	Central W. Africa
Moustached monkey	*Cercopithecus cephus*	Central W. Africa
Dent's monkey	*Cercopithecus denti*	Zaire
Diana monkey	*Cercopithecus diana*	Central W. Africa
Silver monkey	*Cercopithecus doggetti*	E. Africa
Dryas monkey	*Cercopithecus dryas*	Zaire
Red-bellied monkey	*Cercopithecus erythrogaster*	Nigeria
Red-eared nose-spotted monkey	*Cercopithecus erythrotis*	Central W. Africa
Golden monkey	*Cercopithecus kandti*	Central Africa
Owl-faced monkey	*Cercopithecus hamlyni*	Central Africa
L'Hoest's monkey	*Cercopithecus l'hoesti*	Central Africa
Lowe's mona monkey	*Cercopithecus lowei*	Central W. Africa
Blue or Diadem monkey	*Cercopithecus mitis*	Tropical Africa
Mona monkey	*Cercopithecus mona*	Central W. Africa
DeBrazza's monkey	*Cercopithecus neglectus*	Central Africa
Greater white-nosed monkey	*Cercopithecus nictitans*	Central W. Africa
Lesser white-nosed monkey	*Cercopithecus petaurista*	Central W. Africa
Crowned guenon	*Cercopithecus pogonias*	Central W. Africa
Preuss's monkey	*Cercopithecus preussi*	Central W. Africa
Roloway monkey	*Cercopithecus roloway*	Central W. Africa
Sclater's monkey	*Cercopithecus sclateri*	Central W. Africa
Sun-tailed monkey	*Cercopithecus solatus*	Gabon

182

Wolf's monkey	*Cercopithecus wolfi*	Zaire
Grivet monkey	*Chlorocebus aethiops*	N.E. Africa
Malbrouck	*Chlorocebus cynosuros*	W. Africa
Bale Mountains vervet	*Chlorocebus djamdjamensis*	Ethiopia
Vervet monkey	*Chlorocebus pygerythrus*	E. and S.E. Africa
Green monkey	*Chlorocebus sabaeus*	N.W. Africa
Tantalus monkey	*Chlorocebus tantalus*	Central Africa

TALAPOIN

Northern talapoin monkey	*Miopithecus ogouensis*	Central W. Africa
Southern talapoin monkey	*Miopithecus talapoin*	Central W. Africa

SWAMP MONKEY

Allen's swamp monkey	*Allenopithecus nigroviridus*	Central Africa

PATAS

Patas monkey	*Erythrocebus patas*	Central Africa

COLOBUS MONKEYS

Angolan black-and-white colobus	*Colobus angolensis*	Africa
Eastern black-and-white colobus	*Colobus guereza*	E. Africa
Western black-and-white colobus	*Colobus polykomos*	W. Africa
Black colobus	*Colobus satanus*	W. Africa
Ursine colobus	*Colobus vellerosus*	W. Africa
Western red colobus	*Piliocolobus badius*	Africa
Central African red colobus	*Piliocolobus foai*	Central Africa
Uzungwa red colobus	*Piliocolobus gordonorum*	Tanzania
Kirk's colobus	*Piliocolobus kirkii*	Zanzibar
Pennant's colobus	*Piliocolobus pennantii*	W. Africa
Preuss's red colobus	*Piliocolobus preussi*	W. Africa
Tana River red colobus	*Piliocolobus rufomitratus*	S.E. Kenya
Ugandan red colobus	*Piliocolobus tephrosceles*	Central Africa
Tholan's red colobus	*Piliocolobus tholloni*	Congo
Niger Delta red colobus	*Procolobus epeini*	Nigeria
Olive colobus	*Procolobus verus*	Central W. Africa

PROBOSCIS MONKEY

Proboscis monkey	*Nasalis larvatus*	Borneo

LEAF MONKEYS

Sarawak leaf monkey	*Presbytis chrysomelas*	Borneo
Javan leaf monkey	*Presbytis comata*	Java
Banded leaf monkey	*Presbytis femoralis*	S.E. Asia
White-fronted leaf monkey	*Presbytis frontata*	Borneo
Hose's langur	*Presbytis hosei*	Borneo
Sumatran leaf monkey	*Presbytis melalophos*	Sumatra
Natuna Island leaf monkey	*Presbytis natunae*	Natuna Island
Mentawi Island leaf monkey	*Presbytis potenziana*	Mentawi Islands
Maroon leaf monkey	*Presbytis rubicunda*	Borneo
White-thighed leaf monkey	*Presbytis siamensis*	S.E. Asia
Thomas's langur	*Presbytis thomasi*	Sumatra
Kashmir grey langur	*Semnopithecus ajax*	Kashmir and Nepal
Southern Plains grey langur	*Semnopithecus dussumeri*	India
Hanuman or grey langur	*Semnopithecus entellus*	Indian sub-continent
Tarai grey langur	*Semnopithecus hector*	Himalayan foothills
Black-footed grey langur	*Semnopithecus hypoleucos*	S.W. India
Tufted grey langur	*Semnopithecus priam*	S.E. India and Sri Lanka
Nepal grey langur	*Semnopithecus schistaceus*	Himalyan foothills
Javan langur	*Trachypithecus auratus*	Indonesia
Tenasserim lutung	*Trachypithecus barbei*	Burma and Thailand
Silvered leaf monkey	*Trachypithecus cristatus*	S.E. Asia
Delacour's langur	*Trachypithecus delacouri*	N. Vietnam
Indochinese black langur	*Trachypithecus ebenus*	Laos and Vietnam
François' leaf monkey	*Trachypithecus francoisi*	S.E. Asia
Golden langur	*Trachypithecus geei*	N.W. India and Bhutan
Indochinese lutung	*Trachypithecus germaini*	S.E. Asia
Hatinh langur	*Trachypithecus hatinhensis*	Laos and Vietnam
Laotian langur	*Trachypithecus laotum*	Laos
Nilgiri langur	*Trachypithecus johnii*	S.W. India
Dusky leaf monkey	*Trachypithecus obscurus*	Burma, Thailand and Malaysia
Phayre's leaf monkey	*Trachypithecus phayrei*	S.E. Asia
Capped langur	*Trachypithecus pileatus*	W. India to N. Burma
White-browed black langur	*Trachypithecus poliocephalus*	Laos
Shortridge's langur	*Trachypithecus shortridgei*	N. Burma
Purple-faced langur	*Trachypithecus vetulus*	Sri Lanka
Pig-tailed langur	*Simias concolor*	Mentawi Islands

Grey-shanked douc	*Pygathrix cinerea*	Vietnam
Red-shanked douc	*Pygathrix nemaeus*	Laos and Vietnam
Black-shanked douc	*Pygathrix nigripes*	Cambodia and Vietnam
Tonkin snub-nosed monkey	*Rhinopithecus avunculus*	N. Vietnam
Black snub-nosed monkey	*Rhinopithecus bieti*	Yunnan, China
Grey snub-nosed monkey	*Rhinopithecus brelichi*	Central China
Golden snub-nosed monkey	*Rhinopithecus roxellana*	Central China
Burmese snub-nosed monkey	*Rhinopithecus strykeri*	Burma

Appendix 2:
Monkeys in the Language

In the English language the words *monkey* and *ape* have often been confused, especially in earlier publications. The Barbary macaque was called the Barbary Ape and the Celebes macaque was referred to as the Black Ape. When, at a later date, the gorilla, chimpanzee and orang-utan were discovered, this caused even greater confusion. What now was a true ape? To solve this problem, the larger animals were given the name of Great Apes to distinguish them from the smaller apes. And the smaller apes were – by scientists at least – referred to by other names.

Confusing the matter still further, in French there is no word for ape. Everything from a tiny squirrel money to a mighty gorilla is known by the single word *singe*. When *Planet of the Apes* by the French author Pierre Boule was first published in English, its title was *Monkey Planet*, even though it dealt with chimpanzees.

There are no fewer than 94 slang uses of the word *monkey*. In most of them *monkey* is used in a derogatory sense, meaning meddlesome, irritatingly playful, destructive, sexually animalistic, or sub-human. Many of the terms are obscure, but the best-known ones are as follows:

Brass monkeys: Referring to icy weather – cold enough to 'freeze the balls off a brass monkey'. The brass balls in question were the ones displayed over the old-fashioned pawn shop.

Monkey wrench: An implement – an adjustable spanner – most commonly used by a mechanic, or *grease monkey*. An alternative theory that the implement was named after its inventor, a Mr Charles Moncky, has been refuted.

Grease monkey: A slang term for a motor mechanic, referring to the idea that, when his face is smeared in motor oil, he looks like a monkey.

Porch monkey: A lazy person sitting on the porch, doing nothing.

A monkey: A racist insult directed at a person of another colour. Used by whites towards blacks and blacks towards whites. The implication is that the other group is sub-human.

Monkey business: Underhand activities, often criminal.

Spank the monkey: Here the monkey refers to the penis and phrase is a slang term for male masturbation.

Her monkey: Speaking of a woman's 'monkey' often refers to her genitals. This is presumably based on the extreme obtrusiveness of the genitals of female monkeys of many species when they come on heat.

Monkey face: In earlier days this simply meant an ugly face, but today, in urban slang, it refers to a perverse male sexual action involving freshly shaved pubic hair.

Spider monkey: Because of the extreme flexibility of the spider monkey's limbs and its ability to arrange itself in seemingly distorted positions, this term is applied to unusual positions in human lovemaking, especially those employed to achieve deep penetration.

Monkey suit: Because formal male dress used to display a jacket with tails, now most commonly seen on head waiters or formal servants, it became referred to as a monkey suit in the late Victorian era. Today, any formal dress, with or without tails, is frequently called a monkey suit. Its usage is sometimes extended to cover any sort of disliked working uniform that has to be worn in a special context.

Monkey's uncle: A 1920s expression of surprise – 'I'll be a monkey's uncle!'

Monkey tricks: A late Victorian expression referring to any irritating activity.

Monkey see, monkey do: Based on the supposed imitative powers of monkeys, this phrase was first employed in the 1920s as a warning that an action being performed could be slavishly copied by an onlooker and should therefore be stopped.

Monkey around: To tamper with something, usually in a damaging way, like a monkey fiddling clumsily with anything it finds.

Little monkeys: Naughty children.

Monkey house: From the early twentieth century this was the slang title given to a lunatic asylum or, as it is called today, a psychiatric institution.

The monkey: A 1960s dance craze involving monkey-like movements.

Monkey glands: In 1920 the surgeon Serge Voronoff started treating elderly men who wished to be rejuvenated by inserting thin slices of baboon testicle into their scrotal sacs. He claimed that this procedure would make his patients live longer, have stronger sex drives, develop better memories and enjoy greater vigour. Thousands of rich men flocked to have this bizarre treatment during the 1920s and '30s, and he even had to set up his own monkey farm to keep up with the demand for tissue supplies. The term *monkey glands* became increasingly popular and the poet E. E. Cummings described him as the 'famous doctor who inserts monkey glands in millionaires'. However, by the 1940s he was being widely ridiculed by the medical profession and his treatment soon fell out of favour. At a later date, it was even suggested that the AIDS virus might have entered the human population via his inserted monkey tissues.

Monkey nuts: American prison slang for meatballs.

Monkey on one's back: Becoming popular in the 1930s, this phrase refers to the curse of heroin addiction. The addict cannot escape from the heroin that, like a monkey, clings tightly to the victim's back and cannot be shaken loose.

Bet a monkey: Today, among gamblers, this means to wager £500. Many years ago, when money was worth much more, it is said to have referred to £50. Among stockbrokers, however, it means £50,000, because it refers to 500 shares of £100 each. An ingenious explanation has been given for this strange use of the word 'monkey'. It has been claimed that it refers to an old Indian 500-rupee banknote that had the image of a monkey printed on it. Soldiers returning to England from service in India in the nineteenth century are thought to have brought this association between 500 and a monkey back home and transferred it from rupees to pounds.

References

1 SACRED MONKEYS

1 William C. McDermott, *The Ape in Antiquity* (Baltimore, MD, 1938).
2 Patrick F. Houlihan, *The Animal World of the Pharaohs* (London, 1996), pp. 95–108.

3 MONKEYS DESPISED

1 William C. McDermott, *The Ape in Antiquity* (Baltimore, MD, 1938).
2 H. W. Janson, *Apes and Ape Lore in the Middle Ages and the Renaissance* (London, 1952).
3 Richard Barber, trans., *Bestiary* (London, 1992), pp. 48–50.
4 Ann Payne, *Medieval Beasts* (London, 1990), pp. 36–8.
5 Jacob Cats, *Spieghel van den Ouden Ende Niewen Tijdt* (Graven-Hage, 1632).

4 LUSTFUL MONKEYS

1 Ramona and Desmond Morris, *Men and Apes* (London, 1965), chap. 3, 'Apes as Lovers', pp. 54–83.
2 Richard F. Burton, *The Book of the Thousand Nights and a Night* (Benares, 1885–8).

6 MONKEYS EXPLOITED

1 From a communiqué, released on 28 June 2007, by the North
American Liberation Press Office on behalf of The Animal
Liberation Brigade (ALB), an extreme animal rights cell.
2 Judith Janda Presnall, *Capuchin Monkey Aides* (New York, 2003).

8 MONKEYS AND ARTISTS

1 Ptolemy Tompkins, *The Monkey in Art* (New York, 1994).
2 Kenneth Clark, *Animals and Men* (London, 1977), plate 88, p. 131
(for the later 1798 version of the painting).
3 Judy Egerton, *George Stubbs, 1724–1806* (London, 1984), plate 85,
p. 122 (for the early 1774 version of the painting).
4 Yann le Pichon, *The World of Henri Rousseau* (Oxford, 1982), p. 163.
5 Hungarian artist Jozef Rippl-Ronai, quoted in *Paul Gauguin*,
ed. Marla Prather and Charles F. Stuckey (New York, 1994),
p. 230.
6 Jean de Rotochamp, quoted in *Paul Gauguin*, p. 203.
7 John Richardson, *Pablo Picasso: Watercolours and Gouaches*
(London, 1964), pp. 78–9.
8 M. E. Warlick, *Max Ernst and Alchemy: A Magician in Search of a
Myth* (Austin, TX, 2001).
9 Werner Spies, *Max Ernst: Life and Work* (London, 2006), p. 88.
10 Roger Berthoud, *Sutherland: A Biography* (London, 1982), p. 269.
11 Andrew Sinclair, *Francis Bacon: His Life and Violent Times* (New
York, 1993), p. 125.

9 MONKEYS AS ANIMALS

1 J.A.R.A.M Van Hooff, 'The Facial Displays of the Catarrhine
Monkeys and Apes', *Primate Ethology*, ed. Desmond Morris
(London, 1967), pp. 7–69.
2 Mary E. Glenn and Marina Cords, eds, *The Guenons: Diversity
and Adaptation in African Monkeys* (New York 2003).

3 Julie Macdonald, *Almost Human: The Baboon Wild and Tame* (Philadelphia, PA, 1965).

4 'Leopard Left for Dead by Baboon Troop', *Wilderness Safaris, Camp News*, 25 October 2006. Location: Linyanti. Observers: Thuto Moutloatse and Iris Pfeiffer.

5 Thelma Rowell, *Social Behaviour of Monkeys* (London, 1972); Michael Chance, *Social Groups of Monkeys, Apes and Men* (London, 1970).

6 Personal observation by the author at London Zoo.

12 NEWLY DISCOVERED MONKEYS

1 The Highland Mangabey was discovered by Dr Tim Davenport, who directs the WCS Southern Highlands Conservation Program and who led the team of Noah Mpunga, Sophy Machaga and Dr Daniela De Luca. At about the same time, the species was independently discovered in Ndundulu Forest Reserve in the Udzungwa Mountains as the result of University of Georgia primatologist Dr Carolyn Ehardt's research project, which is focused on conservation of the critically endangered Sanje mangabey endemic to these mountains. First sighted by Richard Laizzer and observed by research biologist Trevor Jones, while working as field assistants for the project, the monkey was then identified as a new species by Ehardt and by Dr Tom Butynski, who directs Conservation International (CI)'s Eastern Africa Biodiversity Hotspots Program. When Ehardt and Davenport became aware in October 2004 of the parallel discoveries in their two projects, the two teams then joined forces to write an article for *Science*.

13 INTELLIGENT MONKEYS

1 'The Monkey and the Cat' (French title, *Le Singe et le chat*) is best known as a fable adapted by Jean de La Fontaine that appeared in the second edition of his *Fables choisies* in 1679 (book IX, no. 17).

2 Susan Perry and Joseph H. Manson, *Manipulative Monkeys: The Capuchins of Lomas Barbudal* (Cambridge, MA, 2008).

APPENDIX 1: CLASSIFICATION

1 Conrad Gesner, *Icones Animalium* (1560), pp. 91–7.
2 Edward Topsel, *The History of Four-footed Beasts* (London, 1658), pp. 2–16.
3 H. O. Forbes, *A Handbook to the Primates* (London, 1896).
4 G. B. Corbet and J. E. Hill, *A World List of Mammalian Species* (3rd edn, Oxford, 1991).
5 Don E. Wilson and DeeAnn M. Reeder, *Mammal Species of the World* (3rd edn, Baltimore, MD, 2005).

Bibliography

Aldrovandus, Ulysses, *De quadrupedibus digitatis viviparis* (Bologna, 1640)

Burton, Richard. F., *The Book of the Thousand Nights and a Night* (Benares, 1885–8)

Chance, Michael, *Social Groups of Monkeys, Apes and Men* (London, 1970)

Corbet, G. B., and J. E. Hill, *A World List of Mammalian Species* (3rd edn, Oxford, 1991)

Curtis, Deborah J., and Joanna M. Setchell, eds, *Field and Laboratory Methods in Primatology: A Practical Guide* (Cambridge, 2011)

DeVore, Irven, ed., *Primate Behavior* (New York, 1965)

Elliot, D. G., *A Review of the Primates*, 3 vols (New York, 1912)

Forbes, H. O., *A Handbook to the Primates* (London, 1896)

Gesner, Konrad, *Historiae Animalium* (Zurich, 1587)

Glenn, Mary E., and Marina Cords, eds, *The Guenons: Diversity and Adaptation in African Monkeys* (New York, 2003)

Groves, Colin, *Primate Taxonomy* (Washington, DC, 2001)

Hill, W. C. Osman, *Primates: Comparative Anatomy and Taxonomy*, 8 vols (Edinburgh, 1953–74)

Janson, H. W., *Apes and Ape Lore in the Middle Ages and the Renaissance* (London, 1952)

Kavanagh, Michael, *A Complete Guide to Monkeys, Apes and Other Primates* (London, 1983)

Macdonald, Julie, *Almost Human: The Baboon Wild and Tame* (Philadelphia, PA, 1965)

McDermott, William C., *The Ape in Antiquity* (Baltimore, MD, 1938)

Morris, Desmond, ed., *Primate Ethology* (London, 1967)
—, and Ramona Morris, *Men and Apes* (London, 1965)
Napier, J. R., and P. H. Napier, *A Handbook of Living Primates* (London, 1967)
—, *The Natural History of the History of Primates* (London, 1985)
Perry, Susan, and Joseph H. Manson, *Manipulative Monkeys: The Capuchins of Lomas Barbudal* (Cambridge, MA, 2008)
Presnall, Judith Janda, *Capuchin Monkey Aides* (New York, 2003)
Preston-Mafham, Ken, and Rod Preston-Mafham, *Primates of the World* (London, 1992)
Redmond, Ian, *Primates of the World* (London, 2010)
Rowe, Noel, *The Pictorial Guide to the Living Primates* (New York, 1996)
Rowell, Thelma, *Social Behaviour of Monkeys* (London, 1972)
Sanderson, Ivan T., *The Monkey Kingdom* (London, 1957)
Schultz, Adolph H., *The Life of Primates* (London, 1969)
Tompkins, Ptolemy, *The Monkey in Art* (New York, 1994)
Topsell, Edward, *The History of Four-footed Beastes . . .* (London, 1658)
Wilson, Don E., and DeeAnn M. Reeder, *Mammal Species of the World* (3rd edn, Baltimore, MD, 2005)
Wolfheim, Jaclyn H., *Primates of the World* (Seattle, WA, 1983)

Associations and Websites

THE AMERICAN SOCIETY OF PRIMATOLOGISTS
www.asp.org
An educational and scientific organization that aims to understand, conserve and inform about non-human primates.

APE ACTION AFRICA
www.apeactionafrica.org
Committed to primate conservation in Cameroon through direct action to help not only great apes but also baboons, drills, mandrills, guenons and mangabeys.

CERCOPAN SANCTUARY
www.cercopan.org
A non-profit, non-government organization based in Cross River State, Nigeria, conserving Nigeria's primates, especially guenons and mangabeys.
Location: Calabar, Cross River State, Nigeria
Email: cercopan@compuserve.com

THE COLOBUS TRUST
www.colobustrust.org
A non-profit organization established in 1997 on the southern coast of Kenya to promote the conservation, preservation and protection of primates, in particular the Angolan black and white colobus monkey.

THE INTERNATIONAL PRIMATOLOGICAL SOCIETY
www.internationalprimatologicalsociety.org
The International Primatological Society was created to encourage all
areas of non-human primatological scientific research and to promote
the conservation of all primate species.

THE INTERNATIONAL PRIMATE PROTECTION LEAGUE
www.ippl.org
UK branch: www.ippl-uk.org
A non-profit organization dedicated to protecting the world's
remaining primates, great and small since 1973.
Mail: P.O. Box 766, Summerville, SC 29484, USA
Email: info@ippl.org

INTERNATIONAL PRIMATE RESCUE
www.iprescue.org
Rescues primates from all over the world.
P. O. Box 295
Pyramid 0120
Pretoria
South Africa
Email: s.a.@iprescue.org
Also at:
STICHTING INTERNATIONAL PRIMATE RESCUE
www.iprescue.org/contact.asp
M. G. Lobach, Secretary,
Pastoor Jansenstraat 11, 5076 TH Haaren, Netherlands.
Email: siprn@planet.nl

IUCN PRIMATE SPECIALIST GROUP
www.primate-sg.org
Provides information on the critically endangered species of monkeys.

LWIRO PRIMATE REHABILITATION CENTRE, C. R. P. L.

www.lwiro.blogspot.com

In Eastern Democratic Republic of Congo, providing the best possible care for orphaned primates and working to ensure their protection in the wild.

Email: lwiroprimates@gmail.com

MONKEY SANCTUARY IRELAND

www.monkeysanctuary.com

A sanctuary providing natural surroundings for monkeys rescued from lives confined in cages for entertainment and research.

Rockstown Rathdrum, Co. Wicklow, Republic of Ireland

PANDRILLUS DRILL REHABILITATION AND BREEDING CENTER

www.pandrillus.org

A centre dedicated to rescuing and rehabilitating drills.

Mail: Pandrillus, H.E.P.O Box 826, Calabar, Nigeria

THE PAN AFRICAN SANCTUARY ALLIANCE

www.pasaprimates.org

Acts as a link between eighteen separate primate sanctuaries scattered across the African continent, coordinating their activities.

THE PRIMATA

www.theprimata.com

The website provides valuable fact sheets on each monkey species.

THE PRIMATE SOCIETY OF GREAT BRITAIN

www.psgb.org

The UK's national primatological society, dedicated to the advancement of primate research, conservation and captive care.

Secretary: Dr Sarah Elton, The Hull York Medical School.

Email: secretary@psgb.org

THE SIMIAN SOCIETY OF AMERICA

www.simiansociety.org

A non-profit organization founded in 1957 to improve the welfare of primates in captivity.

Mail: SSA, 6616 North Desert View Dr., Tucson, AZ 85743, USA

THE VERVET MONKEY FOUNDATION

www.enviro.co.za/vervet

A non-profit organization in Tzaneen, South Africa, protecting and promoting the welfare of the vervet monkey on all levels, providing sanctuary for orphaned, injured and abused vervet monkeys and rehabilitation for re-introduction into their natural environment.

Email: info@vervets.za.org

Photo Acknowledgements

The author and publishers wish to express their thanks to the below sources of illustrative material and/or permission to reproduce it. (Some information not placed in the captions for reasons of brevity is also given below.)

© ADAGP, Paris and DACS, London 2013: pp. 120, 126; photo Jean-Louis Albert (Franceville, Gabon): p. 155; from Ulysses Aldrovandus, *De Quadrupedib[us] digitalis viviparis libris tres et de quadrupedib[us] digitalis oviparis libri duo*... (Bologna, 1663 [1645]): p. 57; photo Shachar Alterman: p. 152 (right); photo Toni Angermayer / Science Photo Library: p. 6; photo David Attenborough: p. 135 (top); photos courtesy of the author: pp. 11, 15, 19, 20, 26, 27, 28, 29, 30, 35 (top), 42, 69, 78, 79, 80, 81, 82, 83, 135 (top), 143, 146 (top); © The Estate of Francis Bacon – all rights reserved – DACS 2013: p. 131; © 2013 Banco de México Diego Rivera Frida Kahlo Museums Trust, Mexico, D.F. / DACS: p. 128; Biblioteca Nazionale Centrale, Florence (from the *Codex Magliabecchiano*): p. 41 (top right); Martin Birchall / Rex Features: p. 8; Bodleian Library, Oxford: p. 48 (top); photo © The British Library Board: p. 66; The British Museum, London: p. 114; photos © The Trustees of the British Museum: pp. 61, 108, 114, 168; from *Buch der Weisheit der alten Menschen von Anbeginn der Welt* (Ulm, 1483): p. 165; from Jacob Cats, *Spieghel van den Ouden Ende Nieuwen Tijdt* ... (The Hague, 1632): p. 50; photo A. C. Cooper Ltd: p. 118; photo © Tim Davenport / WCS: p. 159; Gemäldegalerie Berlin: p. 110; from Conrad Gesner, *Icones Animalium quadrupedum viviparorum et oviparorum, quae in historiae animalium Conradi Gesneri libro I et II* ... (Zürich, 1560): pp. 175, 176, 177; photo Jack Hynes: p. 146 (foot); Goteborgs

Index